The Day The Children Fell Asleep

By
John Taylor

MAPLE
PUBLISHERS

The Day the Children Fell Asleep

Author: John Taylor

Copyright © John Taylor (2021)

The right of John Taylor to be identified as author of this work has been asserted by the author in accordance with section 77 and 78 of the Copyright, Designs and Patents Act 1988.

First Published in 2021

ISBN 978-1-914366-31-4 (Paperback)
978-1-914366-32-1 (Ebook)

Book layout by:
White Magic Studios
www.whitemagicstudios.co.uk

Cover Design by:
Leo Banister-Taylor

Published by:
Maple Publishers
1 Brunel Way,
Slough,
SL1 1FQ, UK
www.maplepublishers.com

A CIP catalogue record for this title is available from the British Library.

All rights reserved. No part of this book may be reproduced or translated by any form or by any means, electronic or mechanical, including photocopying, recording or by any information storage and retrieval system without written permission from the author.

The views expressed in this work are solely those of the author and do not necessarily reflect the views of the publisher, and the publisher hereby disclaims any responsibility for them.

Acknowledgments

Margaret Hartford...Relation of Frederick Graham Hall Keeper Victoria Hall

Tessa Newton...Relation of Grace Newton Vowell and Lillie Vowell who were both killed in the crush.

Mark Gibson...Relation of John George Gibson killed in crush.

Durham miner's museum

Sunderland library

Kelly's Index 1885

The Sunderland Cottages.... Michael Johnson

One Year of Hell.... Fred Cooper

The Victoria Hall Disaster...Albert Anderson

The Blizzard

Bill Greenwell's blog of Sunderland

The original of Michael Codling's account was donated to the Victoria County History of Durham by his great niece Mrs Celia Costello, and has been deposited in the archives and special collections section of the University of Sunderland Library.

I have used the archives of local papers with The Sunderland Echo heavily involved in my research.

Secret Sunderland. Marie Gardiner

The Royal Magazine 1905

Brian Stanton for checking drafts

A history of Sunderland, port trade and commerce Taylor Potts.

Website Harrogate Memorials.

Matthew Lloyd of the Arthur Lloyd musical and theatre web site.

Patricia Lovell.

Book cover design Leo Bannister.

The impact of death on the family system. Lorna Bowlby West.

The Fays. D. Arnold

Ancestry Find my past.

British Newspaper Archives

Roy and Sarah for urging me to write it 'For the children'

*This book is dedicated to my grandchildren Alannah, Leo, Charis, Joe, Finn, Jonny, Sophia and Poppy.
All of them capable of great things.*

CONTENTS

Chapter 1	The Seaham mining disaster	11
Chapter 2	Sunderland	17
Chapter 3	Saturday 16th June 1883	30
Chapter 4	The performance	43
Chapter 5	The rescuers	64
Chapter 6	The after shock	77
Chapter 7	Identification of the dead	86
Chapter 8	The funerals	103
Chapter 9	The money	124
Chapter 10	The statue and convalescent home	143
Chapter 11	Who was looking after them	158
Chapter 12	Justice for the parents?	181
Chapter 13	Poems dedicated to the disaster	196

Author's Notes

My mother in law, Elsie Reay, (Cummings) despite being the cousin of Bob Paisley the Liverpool manager, was a big Sunderland fan. Elsie lived next door to the mother of ex Burnley and Tottenham footballer, Ralph Coates. All her brothers were football mad and Sunderland was the family's favourite football team. She was born in Hetton to a mining community and was 'in service' when she was twelve. In 1939 she was still listed as a domestic servant although the family assure me that she was a cook for a large family. She married a miner, also from Hetton, who took part in the Jarrow march. She was a no nonsense woman and taught me, amongst other things, how to make the perfect cup of coffee. She would never run down her chosen team irrespective of their erratic form and was a supporter of them for over eighty years; despite the fact the family had moved to Wimbledon after the war.

When a Sunderland fan took his American girlfriend to see a Sunderland game, she was amazed that they 'booed and yelled mean things at their own players' She resorted to shouting at the irate fans 'Leave them alone, they are doing their best.' It wasn't until a few months later, when she found herself abusing the team when they failed to score even one goal. 'You bunch of ...... not even a shot on target.' Only then did she realise it was allowed to hate, yet love, your own team. But not my Elsie, through thick and thin, it was always Sunderland.

A quote from one owner gives you some idea of what she felt.

The City and Sunderland football club are completely intertwined. The two exist to feed one another. It's a truly unique place that you have this one club that is the beating heart of the city. As soon as you understand that, then it becomes obvious that the two can't be pulled apart.'

Her cousin Bob incurred her wrath when she and her sisters wrote to him for some cup-final tickets when Liverpool had reached the final. 'Not one, not even a reply and to think I darned his football socks,' she told me. I should imagine the same kind of anger that was released by all 'up North' when I agreed to my wedding taking place on Cup final day in 1965 Liverpool v Leeds. It was never forgotten as I found out on a visit to my wife's relations over 20 years later. We were sitting in a workingman's club in Hetton when a man walked past, stopped and turned to his mates and said 'That lad got married on Cup final day.'

So because of Elsie, Sunderland is my third team behind Spurs and Millwall, my late Father's side. Yet with all her stories and the love she had for Durham and the surrounding area, she never mentioned the horrific day at Victoria Hall when over 185 children were killed in a crush on the gallery stairs. In fact when I was doing research for this book I realised that many inhabitants of Sunderland and surrounding areas were unaware of it, let alone the rest of the United Kingdom.

Disasters come in many forms with only the victim's identities changing. Miners, (many disasters) football fans, (Hillsborough, Bradford, Ibrox park). Shipyard workers (Clyde launch), Residents of a Tower block (Grenfell.) What is common to most, be the fact that no one is prosecuted or even charged but that the victims of these calamities become (somehow) the focus of anger and suspicion themselves. The deaths at Aberfan in 1964 are always remembered as the 'accident', which resulted in the greatest loss of children's lives in the U.K. When I was speaking to a Sunderland man he told me 'Why do they keep repeating that Aberfan was the greatest loss of children's lives, when it was at the Victoria Hall.' Not that he was proud of the fact but he wanted recognition of the event. He added that he went to one of the cemeteries where some of the unfortunate children were buried, yet after an hour he couldn't find a grave. Then as he moved away his foot caught something, he then realised he had tripped over on one. He told me it was as if they had said 'don't forget us.'

After much research I have a problem with who caused the accident at Victoria Hall and if I call it an accident, then no one surely can be held responsible. Unlawful killing is now the standard outcome for this (see Hillsborough) I can honestly say that those present in the hall that day did not want this to happen but in denying their role in what took place, passed responsibility and guilt on to others. Following the inquests, as to be expected; no one was charged, yet many were involved in trying to cover their tracks to avoid being blamed and aiding others to free them of accusations. This is regretful but understandable, as who would want to 'own up' to contributing to the deaths of so many children or agreeing that safety was ignored for the sake of cash. But such is the public desire to find a scapegoat that brave men are blamed by others to justify their own innocence. It is unfortunate we can't question those involved, revisit the staircase, or discover any new evidence which might give a better insight into what happened that summer afternoon and subsequently what occurred during the following days.

We must never forget the anguish of the distraught parents, who allowed their children to attend a magic show. This was meant to be a treat, which would be followed by the promise of a precious prize. These are the same people who would be branded as 'money grabbers and playing to the huckster.' They would become a subject of comments bordering on hate. To be accused of sending their children to their deaths without thought of their safety must have heaped added misery to these poor men and women. Do people honestly think that any workingman's family does not grieve for their children as much as others? Then to be denied money that had been donated for them and to be treated like scroungers asking for 'hand outs.' How long did the agony go on? Think of the brothers and sisters who lived for many years with the awful screams of their relatives, schoolmates and peers ringing in their ears. Even though nearly 140 years have passed, a relative of the Vowell family still refers to the dead children as 'Our dear little sisters.'

John Taylor, Hastings 2021.

Sunderland became the first football team to tour overseas when they went to the U.S.A in 1894.

Elsie Cummings from Hetton.

John Taylor

Chapter 1
The Seaham Mining Disaster

My Father died among the aching years
And when the force wind combs
The hairy dust I hear again
The hobbled hardness of his foot
Full on the metal of the old pit road
Winding along my tears.
William Dowding

Seaham is at the heart of a string of former coal mining villages, which are dotted spasmodically along the North Sea shoreline. It fits snugly between Tyneside and Teesside and is now a popular seaside town. It boasts a spa that promises *'a tranquil, calming and truly inspiring space which engages the senses and nurtures the mind, body and soul.'* This is far from a description made by Lord Byron during his stay in 1816 at Seaham House (later to be called Seaham Hall), when he sent a letter to a close friend that included, *'Upon this dreary coast we have nothing but county meetings and shipwrecks and I have today dined upon fish which probably dined upon the crews lost in the late gales.'*

Byron was staying at Seaham House because of an ill thought out marriage to Lady Ann Isabella Millbanke. At the time Lady Anne's father owned the property, which he later sold to The Marquis of Londonderry in 1824. They were married in 1816 but their marriage lasted for just one year. In April of the same year Byron conveniently left England never to return. Lady Byron did not dwell too much on this apparent set back and soon established herself as a brilliant Mathematician (It didn't take her long to solve that particular problem.)

On a rather chilly evening, shadowy figures could be made out making their way towards the Seaham mine. It was the usual recognisable stream of miners winding their way up to the pit entrance. The noise of their boots echoed around the village warning women in their cottages that one shift had ended and another was beginning.

George Roper and his son John were both coal hewers, men who extracted coal directly from the coalface. The wage for their labour was about 5 to 6 shillings a day. This payment fluctuated depending on the market rate for coal and they would be required to accept a cut in wages to allow for this. George Roper lived in Cornish Street with his wife and family, aptly named because it was originally built for the influx of migrant workers from Cornwall. John Roper had recently got married and lived in Post Office Street with Mary Jayne, his 19-year-old wife, who was one of eight children. The pair made their way to the Seaham mine on Wednesday 7th of September 1880 to start their ten pm shift. However their thoughts were not with work as they shuffled noisily, with others, to the pit entrance. On their mind was the next big event in the town's social calendar, the Seaham's Annual Flower Show, to be held in the grounds of Seaham Hall from Thursday September 9 to Sunday the 11th. The 5th.Marquess himself, a rather shy and unassuming man who suffered with gout, was to make one of his rare visits in order to present the prizes. Indeed he was to honour the town, his parents had founded, with his presence for an entire week. As it turned out he was to stay for a good deal longer than he anticipated. Many of the miners at Seaham Colliery had entries in the show and some of these men swapped shifts with those disinterested in horticultural affairs in order that they would be free to attend. It was to prove a fateful decision for those who should have been working on the Tuesday/Wednesday night and for those who ended up working when ordinarily they would have been safely at home sound asleep. The Ropers had special reason to attend, as they were members of the 2nd Durham Artillery Volunteers. One of which was Thomas Hindson a fellow miner who was being presented with the coveted Queens Cup donated by Queen Victoria. The award was for being top marksmen in the 64-pounder gun section at the recent prestige National Artillery Association competition at Shoeburyness.

It was an exciting time for the miners from this colliery as many of them, had exhibits to display, so jokes were shared on the way down in the cage, boasting about the size of their blooms and vegetables. The cultivation of these products was made possible, as they were allocated plots of land to cultivate alongside their houses. The then Marquis allowed them to live rent-free whilst they worked for him at his Seaham mine.

Two hundred and thirty one men were situated below ground, as this was a maintenance shift, so luckily there were not the usual 500 men deployed. All was well with the world until at 2.20a.m a large explosion erupted in the mine. This was heard in the colliery village, with ornaments rattling and falling from mantelshelves. The explosion was so great that mariners on ships in the harbour heard it and looked immediately towards the mine. Miners, on the night shift in Murton Colliery over a mile away felt the shock and heard the rumble of noise. The explosion soon prompted large crowds to gather around the pit shafts, frantically trying to find out what had caused the explosion and fearing for the plight of the miners working below. Rescue parties were formed, with many men who were due on the next shift volunteering. Families comforted each other hoping for the best but, like most mining communities fearing the worst. Isabella Roper was busy trying to reassure her newly wed daughter in law that both their husbands would be rescued soon. She was also trying to cover up her own fear and consoling her five children Mary, Isabella, Sarah, William and Margaret who had been woken by the blast. They gathered closely, embracing each other for support. These were worrying times for everyone involved with such an explosion, as there had to be casualties. It wasn't long before over 12,000 people had gathered at the site from the surrounding areas. The relatives formed the front line of the crowd straining to hear any voices or movement from the pit. The news was not good, in all 164 men and boys were killed in the explosion including George Roper, his son John and their friend Thomas Hindson the village marksman. George Roper's body was discovered over two weeks after the explosion on the 20th of September. The cause of death was the afterdamp (a mixture of lethal gases colourless and deadly). He was found among a group of bodies who had died in a variety of positions, some on their back, others on their sides and a number on their knees with their heads close to the floor, as if in a praying position. His son John George was found three days later, cause of death was once again the afterdamp, He was found in a group of twenty bodies sitting huddled together. They had tried to seal the gaps where the gas was seeping through with canvas, held in position with stones. It would appear this helped the miners to achieve several more hours of life. Trapped miners had time to leave pitiful messages scrawled on pieces of card and wood they included

Oh what an awful position we are in. Michael Smith

Bless the lord we have had a jolly prayer meeting. Every man is ready for glory.

There was unfortunately a delay in the identification of Thomas Hindson as he was one of the last to be discovered. His body was badly decomposed and his wife refused to *'recognise'* him. He was recognised after a year had passed from a tattoo on his arm.

To add more sadness to the Roper family because of the time lapse between the discoveries of the bodies they had to endure two funerals nine days apart. George Roper was buried in Christchurch cemetery on the 21st of September whilst John was buried on the 30th. The happy band of Durham Volunteers, who were eagerly looking forward to the show and the presentation, lost a total of 26 men. The problems that arose with the rescue mission resulted in a delay of a year before the last bodies were brought to the surface and the burials could take place. The Seaham Colliery disaster created a national interest and sympathy for the families. Queen Victoria telegraphed from Balmoral, and the Home Secretary came to Seaham. As a result of the explosion there were 107 widows, two mothers and 259 children without their breadwinners. A Relief Fund raised over £13,000. The Queen chipped in £100. It is not clear whether or not the Londonderry family contributed to the sum. Probably they did not (at least not publicly) for this would have created a dangerous precedent both for them and other mine owners. Interestingly the oldest miner to die in the explosion was a seventy-year-old Thomas Cummings, my mother in law's maiden name. (Late into the 1920s there were still widows receiving relief money from the fund.) The village and most of its inhabitants were gone by 1960. Now there is a great open space where Seaham Colliery had stood for 150 years.

Isabella Roper initially moved her family to North John Street in Dawdon, as she was no longer entitled to a colliery cottage. Her daughter in law Mary Jane moved close by in Back John Street, (In some lists Mary is noted as having a baby). Isabella received compensation from the Seaham mine, which consisted of, a lump sum of £5, plus 13 shillings a week for her children. She decided that a change of scenery would help the family and decided to move to 12, East Cross Street in Sunderland, less than 6 miles north of Seaham. She and her children would no longer have to view the mine that had caused so much heartache to them. The move enabled her to be closer to her sister for comfort and support, without realising that another dark day was waiting for her and an innocent member of her tight knit family.

John Taylor

Chapter 2
Sunderland

I walked around town at night and saw nothing but wretchedness and misery in the poorer districts. Just about midnight, I walk around the notorious and dirty quarters of our city. Dirty and ragged females are seen standing in motley groups. Filthy and obscene language is the rule and not the exception. Lazy and ill looking creatures, the worst possible type of mankind are loafing about or indulging in their greatest delight and pastime, a quarrel and a fight.

William Dunn's diary entry in the 19c a typical judgement of working class lives by a middle class privileged individual.

Originally the Borough of Sunderland was split into three main areas Sunderland East and West, Bishopwearmouth North and South and Monkwearmouth; they had been incorporated in 1835. In the 1870s the town was beginning to sort themselves out; this was partly forced upon them by the 1875 public health act requesting the need for provisions of sewers and clean water. It was noticed that although they had over 12,000 children of school age in the area, only half were receiving education. Local businesses had tried to alleviate the problem by opening schools for their worker's children, like shipbuilder Sir James Laing who provided 'instruction' for the children of his workforce. It was probably more of an industrial education so that he had a readily prepared workforce for the future. The great and the good worked out, by using simple maths, that they had to build another six schools to take a thousand pupils each. QED. Another matter that came under scrutiny was the fact that the average household in the district had seven occupants each sharing one toilet. The total effect was that most working class families were living in squalor. As in many industrial towns the highest absenteeism in schools was on a Monday, when older girls were kept home to help their Mother with the younger children while the laundry and household duties were being carried out. (Coal was rarely delivered on a Monday) Illnesses such as measles, whooping cough, scarlet fever, and smallpox was common. In 1884, 397 children and adults died of measles alone. It was also difficult to enforce the isolation of smallpox sufferers as many hotels and boarding houses refused to report cases in the fear that they would be closed, causing them to lose revenue. Parents were often reluctant to allow their children to go to hospital. There was a case where two very ill young children were left alone in a cold room while their parents were out looking for work. *'To feed the children.'*

To improve health and give residents the opportunity of 'fresh air to walk in' (It was still believed by some medical men that bad smells inhaled by children caused illness.) The council purchased some land from the Mowbray family and turned it into a park. It was to be called, quite rightly Mowbray Park, a lake and terrace were added and later in 1879, a Museum and Library. It was popular with the local children giving them an open place to play, it became known as the people's park. Not everybody was over enthusiastic about the improvements in the town and felt more should be done. The letter page in a local paper in 1883 let locals know what one inhabitant thought of certain areas.

All around our town the children can escape to the lanes and open places. But what about the mass of children living in parts contiguous to High street from east to west? They play in the street. They run hazardous risks of contusions and instant death from grimy morning to blatant evening. Hurried to school mid the din. Small coal man whose cadence deep, drowned by shriller notes of chimney sweeps. They spend the day with games of jags, holey, or cappy. Surrounded by brawling, drunken, ne'er-do-wells, and other adjuncts of the gutter. Let anyone of humane temperament attempt a drive in our crowded streets, and he will find the town literally swarming with children and lounging people—aimless, hand-pocketed, purposeless stupids who never read a book. Shall the children of our town grow up with imitation of these gutter trotters forever?

It would seem she was related to the Newcastle diary writer. I love the language of the time, 'gutter trotters' excellent. But something had to be done for the squalor, which some families were living in. Despite having to share kitchens, toilets, and water, the living quarters were still considered to be fit for human occupation, by some landlords. It is not hard to build more houses for the workingman. Miner's cottages and workers for the glassworks illustrated this. Investment was needed accompanied by a vision.

In 1893 George Cadbury bought 120 acres south of Birmingham and built a 'Village' for his workers, which he believed, would alleviate the evils of the then, cramped living conditions. By 1900 there were 313 houses built plus recreation areas for the children but no public houses as George Cadbury was a temperate Quaker.

Sunderland's vision came in the Sunderland cottage. To help with these crowded insanitary conditions a large building scheme was put into operation and slum clearance began. The idea of simple single story dwellings was introduced to enable skilled workers from the growing industries to live in bungalows with their own entrance and back yards and most importantly their own toilets. These terraced bungalows became known magnificently as *'Sunderland's little palaces.'* The earliest dwellings were built near industrial sites such as Wearmouth Colliery, the shipyards and the glassworks in Millfield. These properties were to become very popular with the operatives to allow them the opportunity to live near their place of work. Many actually bought their homes and Sunderland developed into having a higher proportion of working class house owners than in any comparable towns and cities. There are still examples of these inspirational cottages in Sunderland and surrounding towns today. Slum clearance unfortunately takes time and not the entire city reaped the benefit of this action till much later.

It was decided in the 1870s, that a large entertainment venue should be built, to illustrate that Sunderland was ' a town of culture.' Instigated and funded by the strong Temperance Society it was hoped it would supply entertainment for the whole family. The idea was to pull the working man away from the over 250 inns, hotels and public houses, which were supplying and encouraging them with as much alcohol as they could drink or even afford. The society was rightly proud of their introduction of six newly converted hotels, which were alcohol free and they wanted to develop this idea across the town.

John Taylor

The opening ceremony of Victoria Hall in 1872, was conducted by the Mayor (Mr William Nicholson.) Supported by the following gentlemen Mr Edward Backhouse, (President of the Sunderland Temperance Society) and Sir H. Williamson, Bart. M.P

Sir H. Williams Bart, *expressed his admiration of the beautiful building, That great credit was due to the ladies and gentlemen connected with the town's temperance society for what they had accomplished in the erection of this beautiful hall. He said that from statistics given in the local newspaper that teetotallers had accomplished something still greater, for the consumption of spirits had fallen between 1800 and 1870. If they could only continue the same ratio then spirits would soon be banished.*

Even though during these years many doctors still prescribed alcohol for illnesses; A pint of good bitter for typhoid fever and light draught beer for pneumonia. Although the advice given to the upper classes was to make do with a 'nice claret.'

Not to be outdone Mr Gocrliy MP remarked, *'that he praised the Temperance Society for what they had done and especially Mr Backhouse, who might be considered the father of the building. He advised the directors to turn their attention to the provision of cheap concerts for the working classes.' He urged that, 'if there were entertainments of this character, to which the working man could bring his wife and family to, there would be less fear of his spending time and money in the public-houses.'*

Modestly Mr Backhouse deprecated compliments paid to him in the matter, and thought the architect, *Mr Hoskins, was entitled the greatest amount of credit for his design of this handsome building.*

That concluded the back slapping for one day and they continued with the tour.

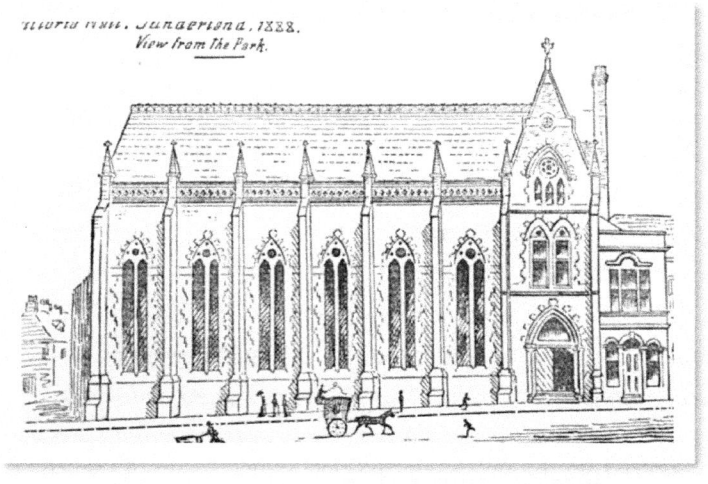

The principal entrance was from Toward road, opposite the park, where a flight of steps led to the floor of the hall, through a spacious corridor. From that entrance level, a staircase led to the dress circle, with its capacious lobby and retiring rooms. The circle was fitted with numbered armchair seats, on the plan of those in the Tyne Theatre, *covered with red velvet plush, and the partition glass that separates the circle from the lobby giving the place an elegant appearance.*

There is a notional description of the gallery and the two exits. The stairs and the dark severe conditions of the corridors were not discussed. There was no announcement of the recently appointed hall keeper Frederick Graham who was *'known'* by the Mayor to be *'trustworthy'* and best of all *'totally teetotal.'* He was selected from over 300 applicants for this obviously coveted position. He became ensconced in quarters at the basement of the hall with his wife Jane. He enjoyed his job so much he called his son Victor Hall Graham. Luckily for his daughter she had been given a more conventional name Isabella after her maternal grandmother.

Although described then as a handsome building, many locals called it cold and forbidding. It was from the outside, a typical late Gothic style Victorian building with vast upright windows. Despite all the finery and ornate decoration in the dress circle the gallery was sparse and frugal. It became the popular weekly meeting place of the Temperate Society and many concerts were given there. The local police band and the Blondinette Melodists, who were described as young ladies with golden locks, also featured. It was not always trumpets and ringlets for Frederick Graham; he had his hands full with some very boisterous meetings indeed.

The Day the Children Fell Asleep

Edith O'Gorman, who was known as the Escaped Nun, had for six years lived in Joseph's Convent, New Jersey, and was engaged to deliver her *'startling and instructive lectures'*

All in all she gave seven lectures spread over three days, which included two for ladies only, which included 'The secret mysteries of the confession' and 'the inner life of Convents'

Ladies only indeed, I would imagine they were well attended, with husbands eager to quiz their partners, on what went on.

It was reported that *'unseemly behaviour, in the gallery, by 'some ruffians'* on the Monday evening, resulted in the gallery being closed for further lectures. This was to discourage the barracker's attendance, by increasing the price of admittance they would have to pay. (They were obviously poor ruffians.) Many people were evicted during the performances shouting out to her that she was a *'fraud'*, some even accusing her of *'being a man.'* She did however tell her audience that *'she had a successful court case against a Father Walsh who had sexually assaulted her in America.'*

Some patrons found her enchanting, eloquent and an honest woman, who would *'stand up against the devil.'* The ex nun raised the temperature in the hall and caused an uproar when she said

'I have found in England and especially Sunderland, the lack of respect for freedom of speech. Men of wealth and influence, who were unable or found it hard to express their sentiments as Protestants for fear of losing the Roman Catholic pound and the Roman Catholic vote.' (Cheers from the audience)

On one occasion when leaving the hall, her coach was stoned. It was reported that the gentleman riding with her, had his hat *'knocked off his head'* but the escaped nun, escaped again, injury free.

Frederick Graham also encountered a troublesome crowd, when the Tichborne entourage came to town. The Tichborne case was a legal 'cause celebre'. It concerned the claims of a man sometimes referred to as Thomas or Arthur Orton but usually termed as 'The Claimant.' He professed to be the missing heir to the Tichborne Baronetcy and fortune. He toured many cities claiming his rightful inheritance, his supporters were usually in high spirits and very boisterous. They were inclined to cause damage to most places they visited on their tour. He was later denounced as a fraud, after it was revealed he had hatched the plan in Australia, following friends convincing him that he had a startling resemblance to the missing Baron. (How many drinks had they consumed?)

But it was not all mayhem and riotous behaviour. One person who visited the hall was prompted to write to the Sunderland Echo regarding a visit he had made. The language he uses would have been common for the time 1883

Sir, Having paid a visit to the Victoria Hall, with the purpose seeing that most wonderful 'freak of Nature' Marian, the Giant Amazon Queen, who is 8ft. 2ins. (Still growing), and in weight some 22 stones, I was agreeably surprised find her not only very well formed in figure, but also most prepossessing in feature, with a very pleasing expression, and altogether a young lady whom every intelligent person in Sunderland should by all means visit. I may say she does not 'stoop' as some have been led to suppose, but carries her height and weight in an erect posture: all persons of her great size naturally move about slowly, and with great care. She is very sensitive, and therefore visitors of which should give every encouragement to her, I am sure, she will thoroughly appreciate.

Her name was Pauline Marie Elisabeth Wedde and she was born in Germany. She toured in England, France and Ireland.

By coincidence General Tom Thumb and Commodore Knott (who was best man at Tom's wedding) also appeared at the Victoria Hall on their last tour of England. Their manager was told that 'the General would have to speak up to be heard in such a large theatre. He quickly replied *'Mr Thumb has played in bigger emporiums and to larger audiences than here tonight.* The General was a described as a brilliant entertainer and was less than three foot tall when he died.

Despite these uplifting events the proposal to supply entertainment for the working classes seemed to have 'fallen flat.' Elsewhere lectures were given for the ladies of the town, which brought this piece of practical advice from a local woman, who praised the introduction of cookery lessons which allowed working men to come home to a dinner both well cooked, tempting and easy on the digestion but added

Seeing that there are going to be lessons given in cookery, 1 should like them not to forget there is a great difference between the upper class and the working classes, Workingmen have not got the income that the better class of people have, so that they cannot afford to spend more on food than is necessary. Therefore I should suggest that some of these lessons be given to the cheapest and best joints and how to prepare them properly and cheaply; also, different kinds of broths and soups, good substantial puddings and pies, with a cheap and light cake.

On the other end of the social class, a Helen Fisher of Bridge Street was offering advice to would be employers of servants, pointing out there were a large number of poor respectable girls who wanted to become domestic servants. Unfortunately they didn't have or afford the necessary garments and asked.

Can nothing be done to give these young girls a fair start in life? If ladies would only assist them when they are anxious to enter service, and give them kind word of encouragement, we should not have such a scarcity of good domestic servants, and many poor girls would be saved from degradation and ruin.

I would imagine the last thing Sunderland desired for young girls was degradation and ruin. Perhaps money to buy suitable clothes would have been more beneficial than a kind word. Everyday complaints, such as noise pollution, were sent to the local paper. A Sunderland man protested about the Police band passing by and upsetting his sick wife in her bed, while the Salvation Army had *'the courtesy to stop playing as they passed.'* (God moves in mysterious ways)

There were a couple of reports of battered women; one was described as 'trifling' by the Magistrate. (Just a small battering then) Two landlords were accused of overcrowding rooms with lodgers both were fined 15 shillings.

Maris Korbes a dressmaker sought damages for breach of promise for £300 against a Clothier called George Stephen.

A more colourful and pleasant view of Sunderland's town moor was described in the mid 1800s

Over the moor women are spreading their washing of clothes on the grass. There is a breeze blowing from the southwest and as every piece of washing is laid down, a stone is placed to prevent it blowing away. Then when all is laid, the mother leaves a small girl or boy to watch them and to shelter them from the wind, the clothes basket is set on edge, where inside the little waiters sit.

Looking over to the beach we can see lady bathers either in tents they can rent for two pence for dressing and undressing or under close to the banks edge. Gentlemen walking along the beach supposedly looking at the beach waves were allowed to walk along.

In the evening the moor had a more bustling appearance both young and old are set loose. Some of the young go to the horse pond to sail ships. Some are playing 'Stealy Claithes' 'Spel an Ore' and 'Buckstick' Some are flying kites and playing with bats.

The environment was improving albeit slowly and progress was coming. Production of wooden made boats was disappearing and steel based boats were in production. Men eager to work travelled from Cornwall, driven by the loss of employment in their tin mines. Steel workers came from the West Midlands; men who were not afraid of hard work arrived from Scotland and Ireland. Seeking a better life for their family that the promise of steady employment could bring.

The town now had a football team, sporting red and white, which would bring them many highs and just as many lows. Elsewhere in the world the gunfight at the Ok Corral in America was taking place. Outlaws Jessie James and Billy the Kid had been shot and Sitting Bull the great Indian Chief surrendered. Oxford won the 40th boat race. Zoedone was successful in the Grand National ridden by Count Kinsky. Blackburn Olympic became the first professional and Northern team to win the F.A. Cup they beat Old Etonians 2-1 after extra time. No gunfight in Sunderland but hope of better times to come with a better standard of living for the workingman. The future also brought heartbreak; it had started to visit six miles south of Sunderland in the popular mining village called Seaham. It was now moving slowly north towards the busy junction of Toward Road and Laura Street and stopped where the much-vaunted Victoria Hall stood. Unfortunately for the ex mining Roper family it was shadowing them and they would meet up on a sunny day on *June 16th 1883.*

❧❧❧

Chapter 3
Saturday 16th June 1883

The population of Sunderland in 1883 was just over 120,000 and the death rate for children 0-5 was 62%, for the age group of 5-15 it was 12%.

The average height of a five-year-old child was 41 inches.

Saturday June 16th 1883 Sunderland.

A huge wave of excitement and expectancy was sweeping the streets of Sunderland on that warm Saturday in June. Children from all over the district were preparing for an afternoon of children's entertainment with the possibility of a prize at the end of the show. Along the streets the same ritual was being carried out. The children were dressed in their best clothes and their mothers adjusted the girls' bonnets, then brushed the boys caps before placing them firmly on their neatly combed hair. Nearly all of the children would have to finish some household chores before they were allowed to leave but this was accepted. The eager children were lined up to receive their last instructions and the eldest were lectured on keeping control, then they were released in to the brightness. Most of the men would have been at work some of them denied even a last kiss or embrace from their wide-eyed children.

John Taylor

The entertainment was being presented by a Mr Alexander Fay and Annie his talented sister, at the Victoria Hall Toward Road. They had been on a long run of shows at the Aquarium and Winter gardens in Tynemouth. (Later known as The Palace). His eye had been attracted 12 miles south to the hall in Sunderland and with the help of a local business man had booked the site on the Thursday, for the show on the following Saturday. They had also printed some rather misleading tickets for the show. They were not tickets as such as they didn't gain you entrance but were purely an advertisement for entertainment. These 'tickets' were given out at some schools while others were distributed in the streets. (Although later denied by Fay) There is no record of how many were distributed but I would imagine that once a street knew, it wouldn't take long for the whole town to know. The news passed on by relations, friends and Sunday school members like a baton in a relay race. The children in fact didn't need the tickets as they could just turn up and pay their money at the door. Prices varied from 3d, 2d, with the cheapest being one penny for the gallery. The incentive was the promise of a prize at the end of the show. This was not a guarantee that every child attending would receive one but the children in their excitement skipped that bit.

The sun was shining and the parents waved goodbye to their little ones and turned back to their homes, unaware of the calamity yet to come. Mothers at the last minute refused to let them go due to bad behaviour, while some children spent their entrance money they had been given and returned to their mother to plead for another penny. Their mother refused and couldn't believe later, she had saved their lives, yet lost the obedient one, who had held on to her money. The mothers were only too pleased to send them off early as it gave them a chance to get ready for an afternoon at the indoor market, that had opened in 1879. Just off the High Street people placed second hand clothes ands curtain material they didn't need on to the pavement. They carried out trade quickly as invariably they were *'moved on'*.

Some journeys to the hall took over an hour with children picking up relatives, companions and school friends on the way. A great medley of children of different sizes and ages, reaching over two thousand, weaving their way through streets and alleys, tumbling from doors of houses, dodging horse drawn cabs, joining a continuous sound of laughter and chatter which heralded their coming like a swarm of bees.

Mary Roper 17 with her younger sisters Sarah 13 **Margaret 8** and younger brother William 10 set off from 12 East Cross Street. Isabella 17, her other sister would not be coming as she had arranged to meet her boyfriend, she waved goodbye to them from the front door. The girls as usual were chatting away with each other and agreed that Isabella would be married soon. (She was in 1885) William walking slowly behind ignoring the requests of his sisters to hurry up and was being a bit of a nuisance. They could have stopped in their street at William Blackburn for some sweets to keep him quiet, or as it was such a warm day they may well have saved their money until they came to John Tennant a lemonade maker. It was just over ten minutes journey to reach the hall from their house but as they turned into Hudson Street it was taking longer due to William's behaviour.

Across the river in Dene Terrace the smartly dressed **Margaret Allen 7 and her brother Michael 5**, left their house promptly in the company of their servants, twin sisters Ruth and Isabella Phillskirk who were both 19. The twins each held the hands of the young Isabella Allen 3 who was considered, by their Father, to be too young to attend. (He was a well-known

Monkwearmouth Surgeon.) The twins walked and half carried the young Isabella for twenty minutes and then left the other children who continue to the hall, while they dropped in to their father's boot shop to visit their family. They would leave their jobs later in the year and soon both of them would be married.

The ill fated Mills children, **Alice Purchase 10, Elizabeth Ann 12, Frederick 7, and Richard 5,** left together from 10 Ann Street but on the journey to the hall split up to mingle with friends. Their mother Margaret had recently celebrated her 30th birthday and was now heavily pregnant with a daughter who would be named after her. This daughter would have a successful career as a schoolteacher. In 1885 Margaret would have another daughter called Maria and all three were together in the 1911, still at Ann Street, unfortunately by then she would be a widow.

The girls may have walked up Tatham Street where a group from the Sunday school were waiting and then on to Murton Street. The boys could have cut through Salisbury Street, in their impatience, either way they would have met at Laura Street ready to enter. **John Thomas Swinney 6** had a long journey and when he left his home in George Street he had nearly 2 miles to travel. His Mother walked with him until they met up with Thomas Wilson 12 who kindly agreed to walk with him as it was a bit of a trek for a six year old. She watched them walk away unaware of the sadness yet to come.

At about 1pm Elizabeth Ava Wright of 2 Booth Street breezed into the brightness to pick up her friends **Arthur William aged 8 and Eveline aged 6** of the Hines family who lived at no 4. With them today was an older girl **Annie Redman**, a live in servant, who was going to accompany the children 'to keep an eye on them'. She was a tall, upright girl and was 15 years old although, because of her stature could be taken to be older. She dropped off some shoes to be repaired at 'Turleys ' at the end of the Street, then after scolding the children for being impatient, the group set off. Close behind them were the Fox brothers, **George 6 and Robert 10** who met up with **Emily Miller 9** and her cousin Alice Bailey 12 as they all lived in Gilsland Street. They faced a long walk of nearly forty minutes to get to the hall but strode out purposefully.

The Vowell family didn't have that far to walk, less than ten minutes from Norfolk Street where they lived over Miss Atkinson's china shop but the two boys Chapman 13 and Thomas 11 left early because they had arranged to meet friends, so were in Mowbray park, by the time their sisters **Grace Newton 8 and Lillie4** had arrived at Toward Road. There, the sisters waited patiently for their brothers. Grace noticed **Reginald Jewett** arriving; he lived just round the corner to them in Foyle Street in his mother's boarding house (Annie's). He had the shortest walk of all the children and dawdled across the road with his hands in his pockets to greet some school friends.

In East Sunderland many children had gathered at Burleigh Street full of high spirits and expectation. Leaving number 11 was **John Thomas Proudfoot 8** who waited outside number 19 until **James 10, Elizabeth Elliot aged 8** and their sisters Sarah and Alice emerged. Next-door at 21 lived **Mary Eleanor Pescod 5 and William Henry 10**.Who left as their 2 year old brother Robert was deemed to be too young to go and despite his crying was left behind gazing out of the window (He would become a railway stoker.) At 48 was **Mary Jane Conlin 10** who was going with her sisters Ann 12 and Rebecca 8. The two half brothers, **James Henry Scott and Thomas William Fleming** from Vine Street, which was just around the corner, joined them along with **Katherine McCann** of Silver Street. Altogether about thirty children set off from the street all of them in high spirits and in a buoyant mood. If they made their way via High Street East it would take about thirty minutes to get to the hall. They became quite strung out by the time they reached their destination.

Street after street was filling up, and then emptying, as the children jointly made their way towards the hall. Stopping occasionally to buy some necessary pear drops and humbugs. It is hard to imagine so many children with just one aim; they were not wandering aimlessly but knew their desired destination.

Another crowd was gathering at Clanny Street, predominantly boys. **Thomas Hughes 7** at number five cut a lonely figure; his Mother had died recently following the deaths of his two older brothers in an accident at the Hetton Wagon Way. His mother unable to contend with their deaths went into confinement and it would seem died of grief. He was wearing a coat that his father, a tailor, had made for him; he stood rather stiffly in the heat. Thomas's older sister Mary Elizabeth would keep him company until Toward Road, there she decided that there were too many children and would go over the park with some of her older friends to enjoy the sunshine, where she spent her penny on some lemonade. At number 4 the Kirton brothers **Alfred David 5 James Frederick 9** and Christopher 6 waited for **Charles 10 and James Lane 6** who lived next door. Charles had to go with a note to Dunn the grocer whose shop was along the street, he told him that his mum would pick the bits up later. They caught up with **Tommy** close to the hall and said goodbye to his sister as she left them. She looked back as she reached the park and waved to them, unaware that five would perish leaving only Christopher to return to Clanny Street. The poor girl would now lose her third brother. It would be a sad day for the families of Burleigh Street and Clanny Street who would pay a high price for allowing their young bairns out of their protection for an afternoon of entertainment.

There was a loud knock at 16 Tower Street, which Margaret Gibson answered and discovered the Cave family from number 13 standing awkwardly outside. John 11 Robert 10 and Jane 5 were calling for her two sons **John George 11** and Emanuel 8. They had interrupted her conversation with Mary Forster, a neighbour from number 17, who had her young baby boy with her. Mary was finding the new baby hard work and her husband had asked Elizabeth the eldest member of the Cave family to help out with some domestic duties. Mary's husband was an engine fitter like John Gibson and they had both been 'called in that morning.' Margaret stood at the door and watched the happy band walking away and before returning to her guest, called out after them 'look after Jane' and then closed the door. This group went via Suffolk Street and would take about 15 minutes to arrive at Laura Street.

At number 7 Page Street the door burst open and seven members of the Blakey family spilled out into the Street. William 13 and his sister Jane Ann 11 started to organise them, **Barbara Blakey 10** held the hand of Margaret 7. Charles 8 and Ada 7 were reluctantly put together. Their mother ran an eye over them and told them 'to behave.' Their father, a boilermaker sat in his chair blissfully aware of the sound of silence. He had been told by Barbara to buy a white flower for her, he wouldn't forget, despite him meeting workmates for a pint. (It would later be placed on her coffin) The children met some friends in Norman Street and by the time they got to the Victoria Hall the number with them had risen to forty. Charles could now walk with his mates free of Ada's hand.

John Taylor

Georgina Coe 11 of Wear Street

I go to Nicholson Street School I got a ticket from my teacher and a penny from my Aunt I went with my friend Margaret Dodds

Georgina doesn't mention the Fenwick family who also lived in Wear Street. Their father, Thomas was a stoker/engine driver. Sarah 6 Margaret 14 and **John Fenwick 7** prepared themselves for the long walk. But they were safely ensconced in the hall by the time Georgina and her friend arrived. *'They live in our street'* Margaret was heard to say after watching the two girls come in.

Sidney Duncan recalled the event, ten years later; he was then the editor and proprietor of a local paper The Blizzard

I was only ten years old at the time and I was enjoying a game amongst five of my playmates, when a man came forward and presented us with a small yellow ticket bill, which he remarked would admit us at half price to the grand entertainment in the Victoria Hall that afternoon. It would also entitle us to receive a 'prize gift' at the close of the performance. What remained of our weekly pocket money was soon gathered up, the game was abandoned and we rushed to the hall. The game forgotten as we rushed off to the hall.

The interesting and contradictory evidence given by Sidney Duncan is that a man, who could have been a member of Mr Fay's team, approached him in the street. The man told the boys they would receive a prize gift, which of course was not the case. They were also told they would be admitted at half price, I am not aware of any reductions in price being given by Fay.

You could almost to touch the expectancy that rose from the children and increased by the nearness to the hall. The excitement had now reached 136 Wayman Street in Monkwearmouth .The

Watson family **Amy Hollings aged 13 Ann Emily Hollings 10 and Robert Hollings 12** (Hollings was their mother's maiden name) scuttled from their house where their elder sister was staying with her parents to help in their grocers' shop. They called out to the Athey sisters, **Ruth 11, Jane 9** and a reluctant Elizabeth 15 who lived a few doors down at 125. Their father was a shipwright and had recently been widowed. His elder sister was now living with them to help out with the children. It was her who was waving goodbye to them whilst gossiping with John Hutchinson opposite, who was basking n the sun outside his boot making shop. The children now grouped together set off, their walk was a straight route but it would still take them 45 minutes. Nearby the Rowell family sprang from their house 38 Gladstone Road, five sisters all dressed in their best frocks. There was a dressmaker in their street at number 4 a Miss Thomasin Brown but they were not a family that could afford new dresses so it is possible she had been asked to make alterations to existing clothes. There would be two of this excited group who would later become schoolteachers, (Isabella 12 and Jane 5.) The other three girls were Mary14 Margaret.10 and **Elizabeth 7**. Their mother was pregnant, unknown to her, with a boy that her husband had always wanted; he would be named Robert after him. Robert jnr would later find work as a blacksmith in the iron docks, where his father worked. This joyful band headed towards Fawcett Street full of stories and laughter. They met up with fellow pupils from Stansfield Street School a new school which had been opened earlier in the year and was just a couple of minutes from where the Rowell family lived.

The town of Sunderland smiled and watched the crowds of children settle at the doors of the Victoria Hall, where any accompanying parents or relations left them with instructions on where to meet them after the show. Friends waved and called out to others encouraging them to join their group, they embraced and waited to gain access, their entrance money clutched in their hot hands.

Inside The Victoria Hall a 22-year-old Mr Charles Hesseltine had arrived at 12.30 he checked the group's equipment and waited for Fay by the stage. He could be described as their 'roadie', having replied to an advert in a Tynemouth paper asking for a respectable and steady young man to assist on stage and *make himself useful*. His duties would also include distributing handbills and tickets. He sat and waited pushing his long fingers through his tight black hair. Times vary on when Fay and his sister arrived; he insists they arrived at just after 12.30. Graham the hall keeper said he first saw and spoke to him at 2pm. His manager Wybert puts them arriving at about 2.30. Mr McClelland a 16 year old clerk from the hall's owner's office arrived at 2pm and without knowing if anyone was expecting him '*just hung around*' inside the hall waiting for instructions. (His mother was a widow and ran a girl's school in Derby Street)

Graham opened the doors to the impatient crowd a '*little after two*' and the children were swallowed up and channeled in. The children in the stalls did not have far to reach their seats and settled in a reasonably relaxed fashion. The gallery entrance was more frantic as they poured in, leaping stairs and running through corridors to reach their seats. Georgina Cole let the flow of children ease before entering on her crutches, she was given a hand by her friend Margaret who found some empty seats near the back of the gallery '*away from groups of rowdy boys.*' Following them in were the latecomers, four members of the Knox family from nearby Brougham Street. Jane Graham the hall keeper's wife, who knew Mary Knox as a friend of her children, encouraging them by calling ' *hurry up you will be the last.*' It was only a ten-minute walk but they had cut through the park and had watched a family launching a freshly painted boat onto the lake before exiting at Toward road. Mary, who at 12 was the eldest of the Knox family held on to a tired four-year-old Ann. Eight year olds Thomas and **George W Knox** followed them. They were the only twins who we know for sure attended the show, they never went anywhere without each other. Thankfully for one of them, today would be an exception.

It was market day and the town was awake. Men drifted into pubs or joined up their wives in the park after they finished work. Singers in the town's inns were amusing customers with the latest Music hall song by G.H. McDermott '*Up went the price*' and a newly arrived song brought in by seamen from America '*A boy's best friend is his mother.*' Bartering was taking place in the market place and traders thanked the good weather for bringing the crowds out. It was as one resident remarked, '*a day to be enjoyed.*' The event was in motion but unforgiving. Despite the clear blue sky and total sunshine a cloud was beginning to form over the children gathered at The Victoria Hall, a cloud of foreboding.

Mr Fay and his entourage had given shows before and had no problems; '*Why?*' He asked to anyone who was listening, '*should this one be any different*'

Figures vary on how many children attended the entertainment but we can safely assume there were 900 in the stalls or pit as it is referred to then. In the gallery total number of children vary from 1000, to some estimates going to 1400. This is purely guesswork, as it was relying on what was collected at the door. Many children admitted they had got in without paying and the collected money was left unattended for a time.

At the door to the gallery with children running around and shrieking with anticipation, Mr Fay turned to the concerned hall keeper

'Rest assured,' he told him *'all will be quiet when I start the show.'*

Sydney Duncan adds

We arrived fully half an hour before the commencement of the show but even then the gallery was packed to its upmost capacity with boys and girls. It was a stifling hot afternoon but the youngster paid no heed to the oppressive atmosphere in the theatre.

We do know that at times the gallery became unruly with cockleshells being thrown down on to the stalls below. Some caps and bonnets were thrown not by their owners but mostly by over excited youngsters. One eyewitness observed some boys were spitting down onto the stalls, Fay and his staff dealt with them during the interval. Some families arriving late turned back from the gallery as it seemed to be too rowdy and having *'too many boys.'* Some children who had spent their money and others who were feeling sick due to the oppressive atmosphere, as described by Sidney Duncan, were left to play on the stairs. The children like the gallery were at bursting point, and Frederick Graham the hall keeper prayed that Mr Fay was right that all would be quiet soon. He had never seen this many children packed into the gallery and as he turned to leave, the curtain was raised and bedlam rang out. This blotted out any misgivings that Graham might have felt and he continued with his duties.

Mr Fay and his sister did not disappoint and produced an absorbing exhibition of magic, singing and ventriloquism but the audience had also come for the presents, all the talking dolls and pigeons produced from a hat wouldn't make them forget that.

Mr Fay after his *Hat Trick* threw some toys into the pit to the waiting children, he then yelled to the gallery '*You will have your toys shortly.*' Hesseltine by then was on his way up the gallery stairs with a box full of toys, passing the fatal door on his way obviously unaware of its presence as he makes no mention of it being closed or even half closed. Everything was now in motion, it couldn't be halted, and the roar of expectancy rose from the gathered throng. They got up from their seats and turned towards the gallery's swing doors. With sparse, if any, adult supervision they barged their way through them into the poorly lit corridors and the cruel stairs. Irrespective of age or size they were swallowed up by a tidal wave of excitement. Wave after wave as fast as their little legs would allow them, with some of the younger ones being carried by family members. Wave after wave, without fear, just a vision of a present to be clutched and proudly produced when they got home. Encouraged by the cry of a young man….**'First one down gets the best present.'**

※※※

John Taylor

Chapter 4
The performance

People present at the performance
Mr Alexander Fay (Entertainer)
Miss. Annie Fay (Sister)
Mr Charles Hesseltine (Fay's assistant)
Mr Charles Wybert (Manager of the Fays)
Mr Frederick Graham (Hall keeper)
Mrs. Jane Graham (Hall keeper's wife)
Frederick Graham's sister and/or Jane's sister
The Graham's children Victor and Isabella
Mr Robert McClelland (clerk to Mr Howarth)

Mr Fay names a Mr Frank Raine as being in the hall before the performance. Fay's manager also names him as being present but later adds *'I don't think that was his name.'* A Mr Frank Raine is known by his own evidence, to arrive at the hall after the accident and was named by many to be of great help in the rescue operation.

We can position everyone who was in attendance at the hall when the hat trick had ended. Mr Fay was on the stage with his sister throwing prizes into the stalls. He had instructed Mr

Hesseltine and Mr Wybert to go up to the gallery and distribute the prizes to the children there. Mr Graham was close to the stage ready to evacuate the children from the stalls and the gallery. His wife was in their kitchen preparing her husband's tea. Mr McClelland had left after watching '*some*' of the performance. All doors according to Wybert were open and ready (later at the inquest he was forced to change this to, all doors that he knew of, were open) He also stated that despite being ordered by Fay to accompany Hesseltine to the gallery he couldn't go as he was looking after the money now that McClelland had gone missing. Each one of the group's stories on what happened next would vary by the hour and day. With the exception of the hall keeper and his wife who hardly diverted in their evidence

Mr Fay's accounts would start with him saying that he didn't know about the accident and he and his sister had packed up their kit and had caught a train from the station and returned home. Not hearing any news about the calamity until the next morning. He then changed it to, that he heard about it at the station and returned to the hall straight away. Then he had another change of mind and said he heard about it from a distraught Hesseltine on the stage. This must be the correct version as Hesseltine backs it up. According to Fay he even managed to assist Hesseltine in the extracting of the children from behind the door. He finally said on oath that he immediately went to look for a Doctor. Hesseltine said he went straight up the gallery stairs via the Laura street entrance to the gallery door as instructed by Fay. The exact words Fay added were to go there to '*avoid a crush.*' When the children ran out he was one man against a wall of children and was ill prepared. Graham after clearing children from the stalls quickly realised that something was wrong. He became aware that there was not the usual rush from the gallery.

He ran up the stairs and witnessed a distraught Hesseltine trying to extract children through the gap. Graham cried *'pull the door open man'* then realising that the bolt was fixed to the floor he endeavoured to release it but tragically failed the both times he tried.

The order of the calamity

The following is an unabridged, combination of reports from newspapers at the time. It is a description of the fatal accident and was written on the 3rd and 4th of July 1883. Also included is evidence from children who attended the show and lived to tell the tale. Some of the facts included are somewhat misleading but the rawness is felt throughout the piece.

The scene of what the children encountered on leaving the gallery.

After passing through the folding doors of the gallery a flight of 25 steps conduct to a landing 15 feet in length by 7 feet in width-that is, the width of the staircase. A sharp turn to the left must now be made, and a second flight of stairs is then reached This part of the staircase consists of fifteen steps, which lead the visitor to a landing of exactly the same dimensions as that which has just been noticed. Directly opposite to him will then be seen a door and a window, all of which when open give access to the spacious lobby at the back of the dress circle, and it is well to bear this in mind, as the work of rescue was mainly conducted by their means. From the landing in front of the dress circle door another turn is made to the left, and a corridor of twenty-seven feet in length by seven foot broad, is brought to view. This is fairly, but not extravagantly, lighted, and at its extremity and up aloft is the one window which lights the fatal flight of steps upon which the horrible scene of Saturday afternoon was enacted. To reach this flight of steps the descending visitor must turn again sharply to the left. The flight consists of fourteen steps of the same dimensions as the others we have noticed viz., seven inches in height for each step, with a breadth of from wall to wall of seven feet. These steps conduct to what is in appearance a well, and with the wretched light given by the single window above it is not easy for one unaccustomed to the place to see the door, which leads to the final flight of steps ending at the outer porch. With the latter this narrative has no part. It was never traversed by the unfortunate children who sought to find their way from the gallery; but we may here mention that it leads not only to the gallery entrance to the building, but by a short corridor it also gives access to the main lobby, in which is the entrance to the body of the Hall.

Benjamin Butler aged 12 years old. 39 Thompson Street

I went to the entertainment on Saturday with my brother Thomas who is nine. My Mother did not want us to go but after a while she allowed us. When we went in, the door at the top of the first flight of stairs was wide open. This being distinctly impressed upon my mind by seeing some boys swinging it and pulling it backwards and forwards. After I got through they could swing it from being open on the inside to the same position on the outside as it opens either way. I paid my penny at the door leading into the gallery at the top of the stairs and entered the gallery.

(This piece of evidence reveals that the door could be swung in a semi-circle and that the door was free from its bolt, before the show started.)

The door between the "well" and the lowest of the staircase, will need passing notice, as it will often be referred to in this narrative. It is a substantial portal, apparently of about eight or nine feet in width, and of 2 inch plank. It will be, therefore, understood that it is very solid and substantial. It will also be well to bear in mind that it swings on its hinges either outwards or inwards. That is a circumstance about which there ought to be no mistake, as it was so arranged to afford every facility for an audience to either enter or leave the building with the utmost safety. Unfortunately, the latter consideration was sacrificed to what were deemed the exigencies of the pay-box, which is situated on one of the landings described before reaching the dress circle door. In order to check the inrush of the audience, which might wish to enter more quicker than the money taker could pass them, a bolt has been fixed to the door, and fastens in a socket constructed on the floor of the " well," 22 inches from the door frame. From this 22 inches must be subtracted the diameter of the bolt and the thickness of the door together rather over three inches and it will then be seen that the extent of clear passage between the door frame and the door was about 18 inches. This was fastened to permit only one person to enter at once, and the proper course to pursue with it was to allow the bolt to remain in only so long as the members of the audience were entering the building. Once the house was filled the bolt ought to have been withdrawn, and the door thrown open. Had this been done on Saturday afternoon it is possible that no accident of any consequence would have taken place; or had some of the children descending the stairs at the close of the entertainment accidentally fallen, the loss of life could not possibly have exceeded a number of five or six persons. Unfortunately, we say again, this bolt was either never withdrawn after the entrance of the audience, or having been withdrawn was replaced in the socket, for when the appalling disaster occurred there were only these 18 inches of space left as a passage between the dark steps and the lower part of the building.

(I can find no evidence that the bolt was in position at the time of children entering the gallery.)

Mr Fay's entertainment commenced in due course at three o'clock, and at that time it was calculated that there were about eight to nine hundred juveniles in the body of the hall. The dress circle was empty with the exception of a woman and three children. (Maybe the sister of Graham or his wife) The gallery was almost filled by a gathering of slightly over 1,100 children.

Amongst the latter it was estimated there were somewhere between three and a dozen adults, principally mothers who had accompanied their children to the entertainment. (We don't know the exact number of adults, there is a record of two or more teenage girls acting as guardians to younger members of the family.)

All went smoothly with the conjuring, the ventriloquism, and the life size marionettes until the performance was nearly closed and the really exciting part of the proceedings commenced, namely, the distribution of gifts. Certain little ones were fortunate in escaping from the hall at this juncture. Either they did not covet the toys and little books that were promised as presents, or they were ignorant of the brilliant chances offered to them. But it is known that from twenty to fifty children left the gallery at this time, and passed through the door safely. Accounts differ as to what was the exact cause of the fearful rush that took place a few minutes later. It is known that at five o'clock Mr Fay announced the distribution of prizes, and that some presents were either handed or thrown to the children in the body of the

Hall. Was it this action that alerted the children in the gallery and they thought that none would be left for them?

William P Clair 12 years old

'I got my ticket from my teacher at Rectory park school and money from my father. I waited till the last trick was finished and saw Mr Fay give some prizes out from his hat. I heard him say that the children in the gallery would get theirs downstairs. I was in the crush on the stairs and got out by creeping through a bigger boy's legs. When I got out I told the man at the door he had better go inside or someone would be getting killed.'

(It is certain that the distribution of toys and books caused an intense excitement amongst the children above and that in an instant, many of them rose to their feet and made their way to the folding doors leading to the staircase.)

It was not reported of any attendant or official of any kind being stationed in the gallery to control the children, or whether there were any teachers in charge of the various sections. It is known that no attempt was made to prevent the rush of children to the folding doors leading from the gallery to the staircase. Between three and four hundred children who were seated in the gallery rose, exited through the folding doors and were swept in a living torrent down the stairs carrying Hesseltine with them.

Joseph Hamilton 8 years old 14 Sans Street

'My sister Jane 6 and I went to the Victoria Hall but was too late and could not get in even though we had paid our money to the man at the top landing. We played about on the stairs until we saw a man come up with the prizes in a box. He went right up to the top and as we were following him he suddenly turned and walked quickly down followed by a great many boys and girls

from the gallery. He stopped at the bottom landing but one and began to distribute the prizes. But there was such a rush that he put the door so only one could get out at a time. He kept calling 'Get back get back'

Joseph became a plumber and Jane was employed as an Upholsteress. In 1901 they still lived together, their father had died and Joseph was now listed as head of the house, their mother was with them.

So long as the way was clear they passed on safely, until, streaming down from landing to landing, and passing the door and window of the dress circle into the corridor, the turn to the left from the end of the corridor brought them on to the fatal spot. Here we can only presume that something took place, which stopped the down-rushing torrent of juvenile humanity. It was the closing door. The narrow entrance between the bolted door and the door frame had been choked up with children, and the others coming down had pressed upon them causing the crush which led to such an appalling loss of life.

Earnest Herring and Robert Ball aged 9

'We were seated in the middle of the gallery with our companions William Rutherford and Charlie Dixon. When the performance finished me and another boy made our way to the door. We called William to follow but he said he would wait to get a prize. When we came to the door I pushed it open a little bit more and passed through. The bolt was not in the socket but trailing on the floor. We heard him say get back'

As soon as we got to the front door we heard the screaming of those who had followed us down.

(Dixon and Rutherford were both killed)

John Taylor

George Bolton Dale aged 11 years old 6 Norman Street

I got a seat near the front of the gallery but the boys in front of me were standing up so I moved back to get a better view. When the performance was nearly finished the man on the platform said the prizes would be given out downstairs. After which he went into a box on the stage a brought out a little wax girl. I waited to see it perform. A great many boys and girls sitting beside me rose and hurried downstairs to get their prizes. I had not gone very far before we were very much crushed. The crowd carried me away. A great many beside me stumbled and fell and were trampled on by our feet. Those who had been pushed in the corner made by the door could not get out. I fortunately was pushed over to the other side and was carried out through the opening. After I got through I stood and watched the others, I saw a boy named Charlie Paine fall in the doorway. After this the passage was completely blocked. The man giving out prizes went outside to get workmen to help pull the boy out.

(Charlie Paine aged 11 at the time survived and became a shipyard driller in Sunderland. He married and his wife bore him 5 children.)

One who was upon the spot almost first was Graham who worked at the task of rescuing the dying and carrying away the dead until the last body was removed stated, *'that nearly all the injured and the dead were lying almost inextricably locked together, and that the only victims found standing on their feet, or in any position approaching the perpendicular, were those against the extreme wall those, in fact, who had been the last to be driven over the accumulating heap of the dead.'*

Georgina Cole

Before the entertainment was over Margaret and I played on the stairs and the door was against the wall, until a man came with the toys in a big box. When the crush came I was in in the furthest corner on the inside of the door and stood leaning on my crutches until I was taken out .I did not see anyone bolt the door but saw a man pull the door after him as he went out.

Georgina Cole became a bookbinder and died in Sunderland 1951 aged 80

It would appear almost certainly that the narrow passage and the door had very little, if anything, to do with the mishap. The inference to be drawn from the position in which the bodies were found is that in the dark staircase the foremost of the children, who had suddenly passed from light into this gloomy place, had become dazed for a moment or two had missed their footing on some of the lower steps, and fallen on the landing. (The narrator is wrong, the poorly lit passage, the bolted door and the cries from Hesseltine and Fay encouraging the children to be the first down, were more realistic reasons why the tragedy occurred)

Mary Roper 17 years old (one of the eldest girl to be attending) of 12 East Cross Street

I had my arms around my younger sister Margaret 8 all the time to keep her up but she was crushed against a railing. She said to me' don't worry I am going to see our dad in heaven.' I called to the man outside the door to open a window to let in air as my sister was dying. In my anguish I took off the cap of a little boy and flung it at the man. A boy lying under me bit me on my back. I turned and saw him die. Then I think I feinted.

Those rushing behind them, unable to see what had happened, or perhaps had fallen about the same place and rolled upon them, the stream of rushing youngsters from above, instead of decreasing, multiplied in numbers and force, and the oncomers, being quite unaware of what had happened below. And so on they went; cheering, rushing, struggling who should get down first. Who can picture the scene that was being meanwhile enacted down on that fatal landing, down in the dim light, in an atmosphere that had quickly become fetid with the gasping breath of multitudes of dying children! Gave no check to their headlong career until they were precipitated on to the struggling heap.

James Henderson aged 11 Nicholson Street School

I went out with some more friends. When I got to the door there was a lot of children there and the door was just open. The man was outside and he said 'Go back' I was inside the door and the man knocked me right on my back. I fell and a lot came on top of me. I could not get up. I put my face to the bottom of the door and stayed there about half an hour then a gentleman pulled me out. (This was Fred Bonner the cabman.)

The heap of struggling humanity in the space occupied by the landing, or well, of 14 feet by 7, had been rapidly augmented from dozens to scores, and from scores to hundreds, until the mass grew to a height estimated at from five to seven feet deep. Young children of both sexes were fighting for bare life. With those in the lowest stratum the struggle must have been short indeed. Suffocation would do its work quickly, and, we would feign hope, painlessly. As each portion of the living stream crashed upon that beneath it, there was undoubtedly a fearful struggle. The children grasped at each other for help, which was impossible for one to give to another. . One little fellow, who, fortunately for himself, was in the last of the rushing detachments that had any chance of being saved, saw the writhing mass below him moving in wild contortions, while hands grasped at the wall or shot upwards as if attempting to seize the wall ten or twelve feet above.

Elizabeth Ava Wright 11 years old 2 Booth Street

I was in the gallery when many of the children had gone downstairs. I thought there was a murder going on by all the shouting I heard.

Two little playmates I went to the hall with were Arthur and Eva Hind of 4 Booth Street both died. A servant girl Annie Redman 14 who had gone with Arthur and Eva Hind to look after them also died.

The imagination sickens at the thought of the scene, which, for the space of five or six minutes, or perhaps a little longer, took place on this spot. And the horrors of the occurrence are increased by the fact that the struggle took place, if not quite in silence, yet with no more noise than is usually made by a body of healthy, hearty, happy children rushing joyously from a place of entertainment. Those in the main lobby of the building and in the outer space of the body of the hall who heard the screams and shouts of the writhing mass wedged together at the foot of the dark stair-case paid no attention, believing that it was simply the children departing light-hearted for their homes at the close of a pleasant afternoon's enjoyment. Thus no help was given to the poor wretches whose fight for life was becoming fainter and fainter. Still the children streamed down from above, until more than three hundred of them were wedged together in a space fourteen feet by seven and their bodies reaching nearly six foot high.

Alfred Dixon. 10 Willow Pond Terrace

I got lifted up in the crush while my brother got trod on and was pushed downwards. The air became almost choking. I was nearly losing all consciousness, as though I was going to sleep. I felt my arm clutched and with the exception of a bruise on my leg and a slight cut on my chin with the door. When I was pulled out, my brother was fast locked among the boys and girls and I could neither keep hold of his hand that was wet with perspiration nor pull him loose. Mrs. Graham the wife of the hall keeper brought me some water and for a few minutes I could not walk and did not know where I was.

His brother Charlie aged 6, was rescued alive and carried to The Palatine Hotel. He died on getting there. The body had marks on his face, which looked like the nails of a boot, but otherwise his parents say his face *'retained his natural look'*.

Henry Souter 12 Tunstall Vale

The entertainment was over and the man tossed prizes into the pit. I heard those who said they were not going to get any prizes and rushed out down the stairs. I cannot say if there was a man on the gallery stairs. I was sitting at the bottom of the gallery and a good many had gone down the stairs and a good many were left in the gallery. When I got out the top of the stairs I saw that the door was slightly open, men were trying to open it. The children were shouting for help. Some of those who had gone down before me seemed to be holding up their hands trying to grab the underside of the stairs above to stop themselves. I made my way out through the Toward street exit and had a drink in Mowbray park.

(Henry's brother Edward had accompanied him to the hall but he went home because there were too many children trying to get in. They both became drapers and travelled together around the country.)

Who can picture the scene that was being meanwhile enacted down on that fatal landing, down in the dim light, in an atmosphere that had quickly become fetid with the gasping breath of multitudes of dying children! Some idea of the degree of pressure to which the frames of these hapless little ones were subjected, may be gathered from the circumstance that the fatal bolt, strong wrought iron though it is, *was bent* by the force of the impact of the mass of shrieking humanity piled up behind it. The children were heaped on one another in tiers. They struggled desperately and some in their death agony bit those next them.

Thomas Wilson, 12 years of age, George Street

l was sitting on back seat in the body of the hall. On conclusion the man on the stage said, upstairs to the gallery for your prizes." out to us. At the door where the accident occurred a man was standing giving away the prizes, and a boy had five or six toys and he said him, 'This will never do." He then pulled the door to, so that just one could get oat at a time, and then put his foot behind and shoved the bolt in. Then the man gave the prizes out, and threw some then down the stairs towards the street. I got a round whistle. When all the prizes were gone he got inside the door and pulled the children out. A gentleman at the top of the stairs told them to come that way, and he would let them out by the Toward road door. Then I went to the street. A man beside the door was telling the children to go home, as there were no more prizes. Some smoke was coming from stage where the man was playing the tricks; it choked some of the children and made them sick.

John Foster, Back Milburn Street,

I was sitting at back of gallery, and I was fearing danger, stopped behind until they had all got out, I did not want to killed, and eventually escaped by the dress circle door. A man told me if I went in down the other way I would be killed. (That man was the hall keeper.)

Benjamin Butler continues

Towards the end of the performance I wanted my little brother to go home but he wanted to see the prizes being handed out and would not go out. I went out myself and stayed a bit in the street but finding he did not follow I returned to him. Soon after, the person who had given the entertainment began giving out the prizes to the children in the pit and shouted 'the first down will get the best prizes. I was sitting nearly at the bottom of the gallery and clearly remember him saying this. We rushed to the door and I who sat near one of the aisles that run down among the seats run with my brother to the top and got out soon. But not before there were many crowding down the stairs in front of me. When I turned the corner of the landing at the bottom of the first flight of stairs, I saw that they were trampling on each other around the door that was shut. I would have gone back but the children coming were pushing so that it was impossible. I was forced down into the middle of the stairs and there the crush was so great as to lift me off my feet. Those who were at the top of the stairs could not see the door until they turned the corner of the first landing and then it was impossible to turn round. Whilst in the middle of the stairs I could hardly breathe it was so close.

Anne Hallowell of 5 Aisley street was married to a John Raine a mariner who had unfortunately deserted her. He would occasionally send her money via his brother until he was *reported as dying* in Australia after being dismissed from his ship for being drunk. She had suffered a lot in her life but was a very proud woman. She had instructed her children Annie 14, Ethel 12 and son William 11, to sit in the gallery and not to ask for or seek presents. The children following her orders were saved and they escaped through the dress circle door.

William Codling was an eyewitness to the disaster he was six or seven years old at the time, went from his home in Glebe Cleft Villas, Bishopwearmouth, to Victoria Hall, with his younger sister Sarah. He wrote this account when he was eighteen. We must take into account that his journalistic background may blight his reflective memory.

It began something in this wise. A man delivered a handful of bills outside the school doors on the Friday night setting forth the entertainment in glowing terms and we were all wild to go. After much persuasion the necessary consent was obtained and my sister & I together with a dozen more out of our street were found waiting admission that fatal Saturday afternoon the 16th June 1883. Some of us went into the pit; others of us paid our pennies & hurried up the stairs. By good fortune I was in the very front row. This was indeed doubly fortunate, for besides having a better view of the performance, when it came to the race for death I would be among the last. The conjurer performed his tricks and at the close of the entertainment stepped to the front of the stage with a basket of toys and began throwing them among the people in the pit. We in the gallery howled with rage. At this the conjurer informed us that a man was already on his way up the stairs with a basket of toys for us. So we obligingly rose en masse and went down the stairs to meet him. I raced up the gallery as fast as I could, scrambled with the crowd through the doorway and jolted my way down two flights of stairs. Here the crowd was so compressed that there was no more racing but we moved forward together, shoulder to shoulder. Soon we were most uncomfortably packed but still going down. Suddenly I felt that I was treading upon someone lying on the stairs and I cried in horror to those behind "Keep back, keep back! There's someone down." It was no use; I passed slowly over and onwards with the mass and before long I passed over others without emotion. At last we came to a dead stop, but still those behind came crowding on, and though we cried to them to get back some looked straight in front, bewildered, while others said they couldn't. I was at the side of the stairs with only one boy between the handrail and me. Chancing to look at this boy at this juncture I recognised despite his white face a slight acquaintance of the name of Fox.

This could have been William Rochester Fox who lived close to William, who was listed in the dead.

I don't suppose I had spoken to the lad half a dozen times but I verily believe that had my arms not been pinioned to my side I should have embraced him. "Hello Fox" I shouted in his ear, "Is that you?" And he admitted that it was. I hardly knew whether to laugh or cry, but I did neither, I only came politely observant of our surroundings. We looked down the sea of heads and waving arms to where all seemed to be swallowed up in blackness. It put me in mind of the Railway Station and I asked Fox if it was the Railway Station but his answer was inaudible. He drew my attention to the fact that several chaps further down were getting a ride on the other folks' shoulders and we laughed together at some of their funny antics. One lad I remember yet had the whole of his body above the swaying mass and waved his straw hat wildly in the air as he struggled in agony. Fox and I thought he was very funny. All around us were white bewildered faces, wails of distress, and piteous questionings where none could answer. Fox thought the toys would be all done when it came to our turn and he said he wouldn't care if he could only get out. I asked him if he thought we could sit in underneath the banister till the crowd went away and he tried to get down but couldn't. At that we surrendered ourselves to philosophic reasoning and dreamy apathy.

At the first landing we were met by some men and taken out of doors into the open air, where was assembled a crowd of frightened people drawn together by wild rumours. Soon men began to come down the steps bearing in their arms lifeless burdens, and from the crowd came a wail of grief, while some of them ran off to tell the terrible news which unnerved the whole town, and which in a few hours sent a thrill of horror through the whole of Britain. I had not thought the affair was serious and now I looked on spellbound as body after body was brought out and laid in a row upon the pavement. One woman, I remember, came out carrying a child that she had gone in to seek while behind her came a sympathetic man bearing another. The woman came down the steps with agonised face and dishevelled hair and shouted fiercely to the crowd

"Get back! Get back! And let them have air."

"Ah! My good woman," said the man who bore her other burden, while tears rolled down his cheeks, "Ah! They will never need air more."

I hung about a bit to see if anyone would bring out my sister; but as she did not come, I thought the best plan would be to go and tell my mother, so I made for home. . When nearly home I saw my father hurrying towards me with white face and an apron round his waist. Very relieved indeed he was to see me. He had heard of the calamity while at work and had hurried home to see if my sister & I had gone to the hall. At home he found my sister, who had been in the pit and knew nothing of the disaster, and was coming in search of me when I met him. Of the party that went from our street only one young girl was killed.

The unfortunate young girl that William Codling mentions was Emily Morris aged 7 who lived at number 17 Glebe Cleft Villas. The family had just moved to Sunderland from South Shields. She had gone to the hall with her brother who survived. Their father worked in a marine store.

The Codling family later moved to Newcastle, and went on to have three more children. William wrote this account in December 1894; he became a prolific writer and a youth worker. He served as grand superintendent of juvenile work for the Grand Lodge of Good Templars.

After the last body had been removed, matches were struck and the fatal door was to be found immovable, by being bolted into the floor. (The bolt was found to have been bent like a corkscrew,) Once the calamity became known and realised, the hall was one vast mourning chamber. Mothers fainted away, and strong men in their agony wept over the stark, stiff, remains of their little ones. It was a scene never to be forgotten by those who witnessed it. There they lay peaceful their eyes empty showing no emotion, unlike a few minutes earlier had been lit up with expectancy and hope. Over them and beside them, fathers and mothers, sisters and brothers, lamenting their loss in heart-piercing tones. There was a stillness in the great hall as men walked on tiptoe, as the work of laying out the bodies prior to identification proceeded.

There is a possibility, that as witnessed by Benjamin Butler, boys were swinging on the door backwards and forwards before the performance started, so that the door was free and unbolted. This meant that when children who were forced behind the door would cause it to swing open. The other possibility was that Heseltine in his panic drew the door towards him and put the bolt down or it slipped in of its own accord. Heseltine always maintained he knew nothing of the bolt until later. Yet he must have known that the door was being kept open by something, as the pressure of the children behind it would have closed it completely.

Finally and most importantly, a child's report, although in some areas it was felt that the children's evidence should be dismissed as 'unreliable' because adults and police- had schooled the children in what to say. Yet Alan Parish's evidence is at least compelling.

Allan Parish aged 10 from 6 Wilson Street

I was at the entertainment where all the children were killed and went with a ticket I got from my Master, Mr Card. I saw a man with dark curly hair rake the muck out of the hole with a bit of stick and push the bolt down with his hand.

Hesseltine had dark curly hair

This is a drawing of the staircase and the fatal door. The door or window at the top could be linked to the dress circle where Graham arrived to assist the children trapped on the stairs. It is reported that the children were piled on top of each other to the height of 6 to 7 feet.

ঝঝঝ

Chapter 5
The rescuers

The Hall Keeper

Frederick Graham came under the eye of many after the news emerged of the high death rate. He was the hall keeper and many thought, without the facts, that he was responsible or at least partly responsible for the calamity. We must accept that he was employed as a hall keeper and not what we commonly call a caretaker or estate manager, which would apply today. His responsibilities, according to his employer were; keep the hall clean, do any small repairs that might arise through the use of the hall and open and lock the doors for any performance. In fact on this Saturday his employers advised him that the hall was being used by a Mr Fay for a 'Magic show.' He was informed at 11 am of this agreement, some reports say 10am, either way it was very short notice. He was also told that he would be assisting Mr Fay in extra duties. This consisted of helping with the collection of the entrance money from the children, which he carried out with no problems. Also helping him was his wife, Jayne.

The following report from The Sunderland Echo 1883. It is a statement from Frederick Graham.

John Taylor

THE HALL-KEEPERS NARRATIVE.

The accident happened on the first landing, where there is a swing door provided with a bolt, which, when let down, leaves about 2 feet of open passage. The bolt is used to check the people when there is a rush in the gallery. This door is generally always open when the audiences are going out, but by some mishap, I could not myself say how, some person, or perhaps the children themselves, had let the door-bolt down. The top of the landing is about ten feet from the ground floor. The meeting was over, and the body of the hall was nearly cleared before the majority of the children came from the gallery. Some men, I think, were at the head of the stairs to keep the children in order. There might be about 1100 in the gallery, which is capable of holding 1500 adults, whilst in the body of the hall, which can hold 1100 adults, there have been 800 or 900 children,

Always when there is a large gathering in the gallery, particularly for children, I go to the outside door (Laura Road) to see about keeping the steps clear. That which prevented the children from getting in, was free at that time. Then, who bolted it I cannot tell you. I have not been using the gallery all the week. The children were coming in a great rate, and Mr Fay, sent one of his men, who went down to check on them. They then I heard Mr Fay say, what stupid men mine are, or something to that effect. Mr Fay left the table where the money was being taken and went down, and a short while after that the crowd did not crush so much. There are four sets of steps leading to the gallery, and the door where the accident occurred is a swinging one, and might stand against the wall or either side. About three o'clock Mr Fay told me he was going further up, as he could manage to take the money better at the top. The table in the lobby or the level with the dress circle was on castors, and moved about, so that Mr Fay had difficulty in taking money there, thought he would go to the top. After that I pushed the table into the corner I then went to the gallery to see what crush there was at the top doors, and I found them open. I then came down the gallery stairs to see that all was right and my wife came and admitted a few, taking the coppers from them. Fay had gone away to commence the entertainment, which was then about to open. I was passing down to the foot of the gallery stairs I observed that the door was open. It was wide open against the wall, facing the stairs where the accident occurred. The bolt would have to be put in by some one. It was rather tight. I knew it was essential to have it kept open. I then went along to the body of the hall to see to the doors there. I found the doors there open, and I then walked round to the dress circle, because I had a better view there of what was going on. I saw that everything was right. Then I went again into the gallery, and there I found my wife's sister who had children there, and her principal reason for going there was to see if they were all right. I looked and saw that the children were comparatively quiet, and then I came down the gallery stairs. The door where the accident happened was then open, as I had set it before. It would then be near four o'clock Fay had not commenced to distribute the prizes. I remember going into my own room, and I took notice of the clock, which - at five or six minutes past four. I looked at my gas book to see what was the state of the meter, because I did not recollect whether I had set it down the previous night in order that it might be ready for the temperance meeting, which was to have been held on Saturday evening. Then, again, I took a walk to the gallery gate. There were some little boys there, and I sent them off the steps. Then I walked into the dress circle again, round by the Toward Road steps. My wife was at this time in the dress circle. She would probably walk down the gallery steps, and, if so, will be able to tell whether the door was open or not. Mr Fay's sister came into the dress circle lobby and left the takings of the gallery on the table, saying she would come back for the money. She then went away to do her part on the stage, and she went by the gallery steps, where the door in question was. Mr Fay had two men, and I saw one of them in the gallery. Then I walked down the gallery stairs I saw Mr Fay's sister go out into the gallery lobby, and then I went into the dress circle to see how far the entertainment had gone on. I saw Mr Fay's sister come on to the stage. I said to my wife, that woman has left all the money, you had better keep an eye upon it until she comes back, or we will have to take it away out of there.' A few minutes after that I walked down into the lobby, but I did so this time the front way. There was a table for money there, and one of Mr Fay's man was then at the table. He had been counting up his money, and I said to him, you have a lot of people here, how much money have you got?' He mentioned that £9. 17s 4d had been taken. The first time after I left my wife the gallery door and came downstairs I found a table on the way down, and I put it through the door leading on to the dress circle landing. There was a barrier there, and I shifted it into a corner, so that was impossible that could be in the road. It is there now, just where I put it. After I had been speaking to the man about the money, I went into the body of the hall that was not filled. Then I looked into my own house again. I had heard from Fay's sister that the entertainment lasted about two hours, and I looked the clock to see what time it was, so to be sure that all things were properly ready for the exit of the people. I came out again and went into the body of the hall. Then I went upstairs by the front into the dress circle, and by that time my wife came away to get the tea ready. I cannot tell which way she came, but think was the gallery. I then had a walk to the gallery gate again through the front way to see that all was right. I sent some boys off the steps again, and came back to the same man who was taking the money in the body of the hall. I said to him 'you will have to get the presents ready.' When is he going to hand them out? If he gives them from the platform, it will necessary' for some us to be there keep order.' Then I said 'there is the gallery, what are you going to with the present for them?' He replied, 'He, has just gone up with presents there for the children the gallery.' He was referring to the other man whom I had seen in the gallery first. I said, oh, very well, I suppose they will get them.'

(The other man with the presents was without doubt Mr Hesseltine.)

By that time Fay was with his last trick, and many children were coming into the lobby from the gallery. I said to them, ' You must not come here.' They replied, 'we have paid our money, and want our prizes. He will not give any.' I said, 'there are no prizes here for you.' After I had been speaking to the man about the money I went into the body of the hall, which was not filled. There were two or three boys and girls running about the back the hall, and I told them to be quiet or go home. They said, 'We are not going until we get our prizes.'

I said, 'be quiet then, and the gentleman may give you your presents,' I got them to be orderly and we got them out. I then saw Fay throwing presents from the platform into the body of the hall. Just at that time there was another batch of children coming into the lobby. They had toys in their hands, which they had received on the gallery stairs. The toys were monkeys on sticks, whistles and small rocking horses. It was not more than few moments before Fay had all the presents thrown off the platform, and then there was a rush of children to got out. I cleared away the steps to let those out who were coming down from the gallery. They were crowding about, but I got them clear of the steps. Just then I saw second crowd coming out the body of the hall, and went into the lobby again and cleared them out. Then turned to the gallery I saw that there were again a number of children on the first flight of steps between the fatal door and the door into Laura Street, I went and shouted to them to come down. I rushed up to the door, and when there I found one of Fay s men pulling the children out. I heard the noise of children, but not shrieks of any one in pain. When I got up there round that the door was bolted, leaving an opening of about 18 inches, which the children could get through. This was quite different from the state, which I had last seen the door when it was folded back against the wall where it ought to be. I believe Fay's man had been giving presents away to the children as they were leaving the hall by that door. I believe that man had put the bolt in to relieve the pressure; the man was petrified state of fright and terror, and quite faint. He was standing just at the opening the door, slightly inside it, and was pulling at the children who were jammed against the dour. I did not then realise that the accident was serious. He was much overcome that I took his place, and my first attempt was pull out the bolt. With some difficulty got my hand in. I asked Police Constable Berwick to move the door and give it a chance. I tried my best, but could not get the bolt out. Then went upstairs through the dress-circle lobby, and from it through the lobby that leads to the gallery and began pulling the children through the dress circle way. By this time some men were through the dress circle and I set to work. 1 worked my way along amongst the children till got to the end of the lobby and the head of the flight steps leading to the fatal door. I got hold of the stair rail and pulled myself along, and the men following me were taking the children I handed them back. I knelt down again and tried to pull the bolt, but though 1 used my utmost exertion and was assisted by a policeman, who shook the door, was unable to get it out. It would about hour before the children were entirely cleared out. I was fatigued I had to leave for a few minutes to get breath. Some men brought drink, and I rushed in again. They asked me to come out as I was almost fainting, but 1 stuck to it until they were all out. The bolt was bent with the crush. I could have pulled it but for that I think. The bolt might have slipped in with the door moving backwards and forwards. I afterwards found a box which the presents were kept be lying outside the door where the crush occurred.

Later in his basement room Frederick Graham was described as being *'almost overpowered and detached by the fatality.'* He spoke to a Northern Echo reporter

'I*n broken sentences'*

'Some children were heads down and feet up; it took 7 or 8 men to extract them. The poor children were just past shouting when we got to them. It wasn't till 6 pm when we finished helping them.'

Fay was never questioned on his altercation with his men, which resulted in him exclaiming 'what stupid men mine are' to Graham. What did he say to reduce the rush of the children? Perhaps the fatal door was closed to reduce the number of children being admitted, was this done?

The children were later described as being locked together by arms and legs and it took a long time to separate them as the rescuers were frightened they might break their limbs. There are some people who eagerly assisted the hall keeper. It was also the case that some men who ran up the stairs to help, covered their faces, because of the foul smell and then quickly returned to the outside of the hall and laid down in the park, fully overcome by the carnage they had seen and because of this, unable to help with the rescue.

Fred Bonner a cab driver who was washing down his horse when he heard cries coming from the hall. He thought that the children were crying out for more magic. He asked some boys who were exiting from the Laura street exit what was wrong. They him told that there were some children stuck behind the door. He rushed up the stairs, *'not seeing or passing any adults,'* and proceeded to pull out children from behind the door. He pulled off a coat sleeve from a boy, then grabbed him around his body and managed to pull him out. He saved two more boys then a girl who unfortunately was dead. He said the rest were stuck fast.

Fred Bonner must have arrived after Hesseltine, who nearing collapse, had gone downstairs to tell Fay about the accident. Frederick Graham was already on his way to the dress circle door after Pc Berwick arrived, who then left the scene to inform medical men and to request some more constables to attend.

Police-Constable Bewick number 51 At about 5 pm whilst on duty in the High Street. He received information from 2 young boys that a panic had occurred at the Victoria Hall among some children. He was told the stage had collapsed. On going to the hall he went up to the first landing on the stairs. He found the door bolted to the floor and open only about foot and half. A great many children were lying in a heap behind it, all packed one upon another. A great many of them were dead. With the assistance of the hall keeper he got them removed downstairs. Graham suggested that Berwick should seek medical assistance.

He left the hall and located the nearest medical men and asked for their help. Before returning he told others to go for some more Doctors and then sent a messenger to the Chief Constable at the Central Police station, asking for a force not less than twelve officers to be sent to the hall immediately. As soon as he sent the messengers he appealed to the crowd for strong men to help, about six men stepped forward and went back with him to the gallery door and helped to carry out the children. They placed those they thought were living either outside or in front of the lobby, and the dead were put in the body of the hall, which this time had been quite cleared of its audience. Police Constable Berwick found a girl pressed so hard against the door, her jacket was torn right through. He took her out and she remembers him saying, *'what a good job to see such a nice girl as you' and then he kissed her.*

Another incident that Pc Berwick recalls thirty years after the event to the magazine The Royal was as follows.

'I next brought out a little girl, then I seized and pulled away a girl of sixteen or seventeen about the oldest of the children at the entertainment. Hers was the most terrible of all the cases I saw and that came to notice. Both her legs were crushed and she was dreadfully crushed and injured. Her clothing had been stripped from her body. She turned and her eyes met mine as she whispered ' Oh my mother my bonnie mother.' Then she passed away. It is still one of the saddest cases of all and it is still with me as she came from a family who lost three children.

After he retired as a policeman Mr Berwick worked at the Empire Theatre in High Street West in Sunderland

Sergeant Major Willing, instructor of the Voluntary Artillery. He assisted Berwick in taking away children from the door. He witnessed children dying in his arms and others accusing '*other chaps' of kicking and biting them during the crush*. He took a young boy to the Park Lake and tried to revive him with artificial respiration but failed and carried him back to lay him out with the other dead children.

Pc no 105 Arthur Clark assisted Graham with the clearing of children from the stairs. Then laid them out on 'the flags. He also assisted Berwick in withdrawing the bolt from the hole to allow the door to be opened. Berwick wrote.

'To do this I had to put my oak truncheon between the bolt and the woodwork, which was not difficult as the bolt had been bent outwards by the pressure. Then my comrade and myself got our hands on the stave, two at each end and the good oak acting as a lever, we raised the bolt out of the floor and got the door open.'

This is the only account of the releasing of the bolt that I could find. I know that Graham had tried twice to free the bolt but had failed. This account from Berwick was written nearly 30 years later but he maintains it is true 'as it was written in his police notebook.'

A photograph of P.C. Berwick in 1905

A railway clerk called **Mathew Thompson** helped to carry children down the stairs.

A florist from Toward Street Mark Hutchinson and his errand boy, rushed to get supplies of water, to administer to the children.

Henry Waite a cab driver. He helped with conveying children from the dress circle and placed them in waiting cabs so their parents could take them home.

Thomas Rutherford; for five hours he was active with the bodies, he brought them up to the dress circle and laid them on the floor, straightening their arms and legs to try and give them a less ghastly appearance for their loved ones He confided *' I will never forget the dreadful scenes nor the cries of the parents.'*

Frank Raine who was reported to reside at 4 Howick Street. Hearing of the accident, he at once ran to the hall where he found Mr Graham and P.C Berwick busy attempting to rescue the children heaped behind the door. Mr Graham handed the children out to them and they placed those who they thought were alive outside in the open air. He said *'we all exerted ourselves to the very upmost to get the poor things out from the door. Some of the men who rushed to assist us when they saw the mass of children dying and dead fainted, others were struck with horror and rushed out again.'*

Frank Raine could possibly be the mysterious mason (bricklayer) who was employed by a Mr Thompson, also a mason, who unfortunately lost a child. Raine was described as having 'great strength.' by fellow rescuers.

In the 1881 censor there is listing of a Frank Charles Raine living in Dean Street, his occupation is listed as a mason. In 1883 the occupants of 4 Howick Street were listed as a grocer and an undertaker. Raine could have lived above the shops, although I have found no evidence of this. At number 6 Howick Street we have John Edward Dixon aged 6, who died in the crush, whose father was a tailor.

Dr Beattie was walking down Borough Road when he saw P.C. Berwick running towards Victoria Hall. Once he was there he saw an enormous heap of children compacted together and nearly 6 feet high. He estimated that there was 'over 300 children massed together' He describes that some of the children held their hands out crying 'Give me a hand' Whilst Dr Walker Beattie was hard at work attending to the injured, a man up in the dress circle, who was looking for his children amongst the dead, identified two of the bodies as those of his boys and was so overcome that he fainted away. He happened to be leaning over the front of the dress circle at the time; he fell right over ' the breast ' upon Dr Beattie below. Dr Beattie was thrown to the ground, but fortunately suffered no injury. Owing to the man's fall being broken by Dr Beattie another fatality was in all probability averted. More medical men arrived including Doctors; Lambert, Bolton, Waterson and Potts to give their assistance and medical advice in fact nearly every doctor in the town attended the calamity.

Ken Rooks, who like so many of the people in the vicinity rushed to the lobby to help. He helped carry children down the stairs that allowed them to receive some fresh air and water to recover. (A family story passed down and recounted by his granddaughter Leithia Ann Bell.)

After the last body had been removed, matches were struck and the fatal door was found to be immovable, due to being bolted into the floor. Once the calamity became known and realised, the hall and surrounding area became one vast mourning chamber.

The rescuers had witnessed horrific scenes with many having to seek fresh air in Mowbray Park, brushing aside questions from the general public,, not wanting to relive the horror they had just experienced. The crowds gathered and grew more vocal wanting answers not from gloom makers but from people with first hand knowledge. As the minutes passed the atmosphere started to change and those in charge realised they had a challenge to face.

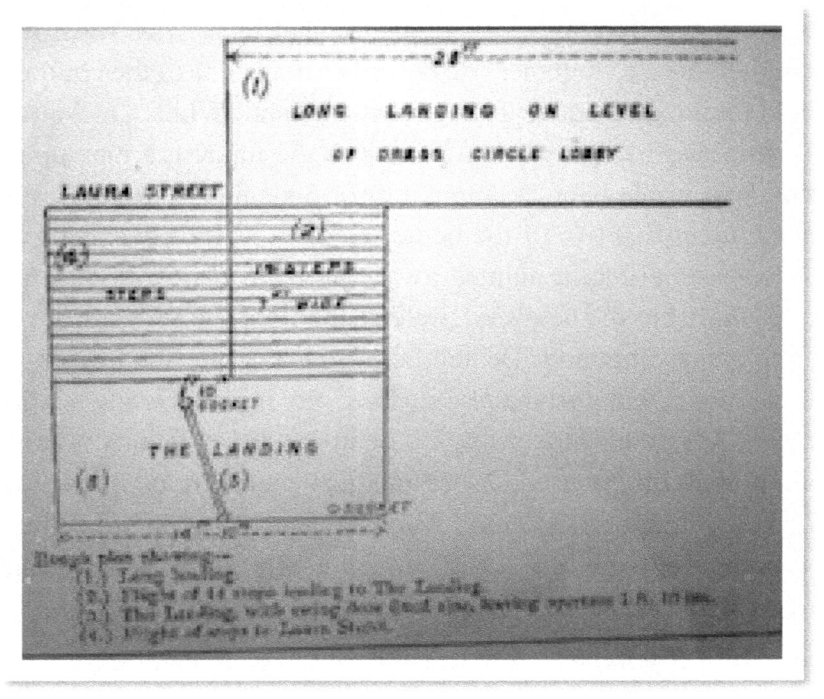

This is the rather misleading drawing that appeared in many publications, including PC Berwick's notebook. It seems they have the Laura Street steps on wrong side so it appears the door is opening the wrong way.

❧❧❧

Chapter 6
The Aftershock

It was a scene never to be forgotten by those who witnessed it. There lay the rigid little corpses, cold in death. Peaceful and pleasant were many of the faces, which but a few minutes before were lit up with expectancy and hope. Over them and beside them, fathers and mothers, sisters and brothers, bewailed their loss in heart-piercing tones. There, in the stillness of the great Hall for men bated their breath, and walked on tiptoe, as the work of laying out the bodies prior to identification proceeded lay the stiff, stark corpses of the dead, ranged in rows in the dress circle and in the area beneath. Faces pale and wan were there; others peaceful and unmarked, as if the last, long sleep had not begun; and many were blackened and disfigured in a manner too horrible to describe.

Later the Police issued a list of clothing that had not been claimed they included; imitation dog skin/sealskin coats, dolman shawls, shoes with elastic sides, Glengarry caps, In a jacket was a purse with coppers, and dapper little caps and bonnets, torn and trampled, were lying all over the place; buttons and fragments of clothing littered the floor; here lay the little blue ribbon which had tied up some girl's hair; there lay a child's garter; on another spot the sole of a little boy's boot torn from the "uppers," furnishing mute but significant evidence of the violence of the death-struggle.

One can only imagine the scenes around Victoria Hall when the news of the deaths spread around the areas of Bishopwearmouth and Monkwearmouth. To begin with the news filtered through word of mouth that about twenty were killed, this consoled some parents although it could have been five, one of those could still be your child. When the real toll became apparent then the panic started. The Victoria Hall was besieged with parents praying that their bairns were safe, they just wanted to get in to reach their children and 'hold them close.' Many were relieved to find their children playing in Mowbray Park; others met their loved ones on their journey to the hall causing bewilderment amongst the children as they were swept up into their parent's arms and held close to their chests. Some parents who had reached the hall had to wait outside, begging for news from anybody leaving the hall and the guarding policemen. Each minute the crowd increased demanding to go into the hall to find their children, with such a small force the police were finding it difficult to keep order. Each one had sympathy with the plight of the parents and their pleading to let them in.

The hour was a most unfortunate one for the gathering of a sufficient number of the borough police force, as the streets at the time were crowded with the usual market-day multitude. The men being not only busy in the execution of their duties, but because of the distance between each officer, it was difficult to get in touch with them quickly. Although the Chief Constable summoned a large body of police, the number available was found insufficient to cope with the enormous crowd of over 20.000 persons that had gathered on all sides of the hall. In fact he had only received a dozen special constables who were just about to come on duty for their Saturday night shift hardly enough to be able to cope with the present situation. The majority of these people gathered were agonised parents and relations, who quite rightly sought admittance to the hall. So great was the excitement, so determined the rush of many of these poor people, that the police force was for a moment overpowered, it was stated at one point that their commander had said *'We are licked.'* There seemed to be every prospect of a second panic and the occurrence of a mishap more dreadful even than that which had just taken place inside the hall. The Mayor, Alderman McKenzie, Alderman Nicholson, Councilor Howarth, Councilor Dix, and other gentlemen held a brief conference upon the hall steps on what would be the best plan that could be put into action in the present circumstances. They decided that a messenger should be sent to the Sunderland Barracks, with a request that the commandant of the garrison would grant the use of a body of troops, to provide assistance for the now beleaguered police force. The maintenance of order had to be observed quickly to strengthen the prevention of what seemed an impending calamity.

A company of the Durham Light Infantry (the old 68th regiment) was dispatched, to the hall under the command of Lieut. Gales.

The soldiers were arranged in a cordon round the front and back of the building taking in the Laura road and Toward road entrances and gave the important and necessary aid to the police in regulating and controlling the movements of the crowd.

Two women approached Pc Berwick who was fresh from assisting the rescue of the children; they were drunk and asked about the children. He was is no mood to waste time on them and asked *'are your children here?'*

'They might be'

'Then give me some help' they refused, so he sent them on their way.

Berwick was then asked to step inside the hall and keep watch over the door to the main lobby whilst another meeting was taking place within the hall with The Mayor, chief constable, members of the town council and doctors. They discussed what should be done next and whether the parents should be let in, to view the dead children and recognise any family members. They hoped that this would help placate the impatient crowd. Pc Berwick was put in charge of the door and only admitted constables, some of whom were overcome with emotion and near collapse. Then he heard a strong impatient knock with a loud demand for admission.

'Who's there?' asked Berwick. He was told the name of a well-known gentleman.

'I 'm sorry sir but you can't come in'

The man answered in amazement *'Do you know who you are speaking to? I am councillor so and so*

'I'm sorry sir' was the reply *'if you were twenty councillors you wouldn't be allowed in. You do as I tell you. I am the constable on duty,'* replied Berwick stoutly.

The mayor said warmly to him *'you are a man Berwick.'*

William Berwick had witnessed tragedy before and was on active service as a soldier in the Boer wars in South Africa. He took part in the Majuba Hill battle where over 250 British soldiers were killed, injured or taken prisoners, so no person full of his own importance would cut any ice with him.

At the earliest possible moment an announcement was made that all persons having reason to think their children were inside the hall had to step forward and proceed with the task of identification. A fearful scene followed this notification. Fathers and mothers whose children had left their homes happy and cheerful only a few hours earlier, scrambled and pushed through the crowd and besieged the door of the hall.

Once the calamity became known and realised, the hall was one vast mourning chamber.

The police and soldiers, with that kindness and feeling which distinguish all our services under circumstances of the kind, permitted the widest latitude to those people, as they crammed the outer lobby, and streamed into the body of the Hall. Some who had dashed frantically into the hastily improvised mortuary, were so horrified by the sight which met their gaze when once they were fairly within its walls, that they stopped, almost as if transfixed. The dead children lay stretched in rows upon the floor, presenting a spectacle that was calculated to touch the hardest heart. Most of the poor little ones lay as if calmly sleeping, with the exception of a slight suffusion about the eyes.

In the great majority of the cases there were no signs of bodily injuries, no heavy bruising. The hands were relaxed, the eyes mostly closed, and the lips often drawn into a smile. Many parents refused to believe they were dead and told doctors to help them crying '*There is now't wrong with them.*' Parents rushed out from the hall overcome with sadness and unable to face the appalling sight, only returning again as if suddenly aware of their duties as parents. In many instances, mothers, hastily treading between the lines of dead, stooping down, recognised their children at a glance, and collapsed, falling on them as if to protect them.

One man screamed awfully, threw his hands above his head, and cried out, 'My son is dead, my son is dead!' Turning sharply round, he rushed frantically through the crowd which was pressing into the hall, cleaving his way amongst the multitude, and it was transparent that in his despair he was intending to commit some injury to himself. Sympathising people who were about pursued him, and gradually calmed down his passion of grief. In another case a man and his wife rushed in. The man eagerly scanned the faces of the dead, and, without betraying any emotion, said, with his finger pointed and, with face blanched, 'That's one, 'and passing on two or three yards, still pointing, 'That's another' and still walking on, pointing to the last child in the row, he uttered, 'Good God! All my family gone 'and staggering back, cried out, 'Give me water, give me water.' His face seemed to turn into furrows deep at once, and his eyes sank

In fact, the scenes of unbearable sorrow that occurred in and around the hall at about six thirty were of a nature that people would not have imagined to have been seen anywhere else. The hardened men of the military and police forces present were moved to tears at the sight. The medical men for some time had their energies fully focused on attending to women insensible through sudden excess of grief, or to men who had for a moment lost their senses when face to face with their children's deaths. Their efforts, which they made to tend to, not only the comfort for the physical condition of the stricken parents, but for words of condolences to them trying to achieve the impossible of giving relief of their grief. Their action would only bring great respect from the population of Sunderland.

Very soon the work of removing the dead commenced but not before Chief Constable Nicholson and the authorities had organised a system of recording their names. Before the bodies were released care was taken to obtain the names and addresses of the parents and the dead. This was hindered as many children had been removed by their parents and had to be visited at home, to certify their name. Most of the poor little victims had been laid decently side-by-side upon the floor. As each parent recognised his or her child, they were lifted from the ground and so carried out into the street, where an efficient system of aiding the removal had been arranged. Many Sunderland cab men had driven to the spot that had resulted in rows of cabs waiting for the appearance of the parents and their children. They were instantly helped into the conveyances and driven to their homes. Among those engaged in this were Graham and local celebrity Mr Henry Watts, whose exertions in saving life as a lifeboat captain had been known throughout the length and breadth of the country.

He was reported to have saved or rescued over 60 people in his lifetime. The last one when he was in his late sixties. His son and grandson carried on the tradition and became members of the crew of a lifeboat.

In the case of disaster like this, the proportion of injured to dead is not great. The crush at the bottom of the staircase, ensured the almost certain death of the early arrivals at the door. It was estimated that over 300 were thrust into the moving heap and of this number, the amount of children saved equated to about one-third. The survivors were suffering from suffocation, shock, bruises caused by the grasp of dying hands, and from the beating they sustained against the walls and stairs in their struggles to release themselves. Only one case of a survivor with a broken bone was reported, this was a boy whose arm had been fractured. (Thomas Kent who later worked in the shipyard) Only a few of the dead with broken bones were identified and reported.

Everybody that gave the slightest sign of life when examined by the medical gentlemen were treated by means of fresh water, stimulants and the usual modes of artificial respiration. Two cases taken in hand by Dr Abrath were treated by means of electricity, and both recovered. In the majority of the cases when a glimpse of life remained, the doctors treated them and most completely recovered.

Those who were suffering with shock and its consequences were dealt with at the homes of the children, whilst others were transferred to the Infirmary. The work of identification and of removing the dead and injured proceeded till after ten o'clock. During this time the lint had arrived and the dead children's heads were tied up, their hands tied over their breasts and their feet were tied together for their last journey home.

Some children had departed from the hall before the calamity had evolved and started on their way home or visited the park fully unaware of what had happened. One distraught mother, who had visited the hall but couldn't find her child, returned home to find her daughter playing in the street with her friends. Her relieved mother gathered her up and covered her in kisses. Her daughter exclaimed

'Oh Mummy we fell asleep on the stairs.'

Chapter 7
Identification of the children

Then came an equally upsetting time, when the parents, friends and in some cases siblings identified the dead children. The bodies were laid out to be viewed, in the dress circle of the hall, others across the road at The Palatine Hotel. In some cases the parents on recognisng their children swept them up and away from the hall to their homes. This caused irregularities as to the number of children that had been killed, plus remarkable as it might seem, some parents in their stunned grief took the wrong child home. One woman saying that only on inspection of the child's underwear did she realise that *'this is not my child.'*

The recognition of children by a friend or relation caused some confusion as the children were sometimes listed with the surname of the identifier. The act of walking past the bodies and crouching down to recognise one of your children must have been devastating. Children you waved goodbye to on a bright sunny summer's day now with empty eyes lay dead at your feet. No imagination of your own can put you in their place, brushing the hair from their small face, then having to say the words 'I recognise that this is …

Report from Sunderland Echo as printed.

George Wanless commercial traveller, 8 Dock Street, Shore, who identified his daughter, Elizabeth Wanless, 7 years of age, was at the entertainment with William Sinclair Wanless, her brother.

Joshua Pringle, Provision dealer, Southwick Road identified his daughters, Ann Milner Pringle, 9 years and Margaret Pringle 7 years.

Matthew Ward, Riveter, Back Charles Street, identified his daughter, Florence Edith Ward, 6 years who was with her two sisters who survived. They were twelve and eight years of age respectively.

John Nipper, Shipwright, 11 Square, identified his son George Stokell Nipper, nine years of age.

Shipley, a porter, residing Griffins Buildings, identified his son Walter Gibson Shipley, 10 years age, the deceased went to the Victoria Hall with another two children, and lost his life.

Thomas McKeever, labourer, lodging in Society Lace, said John McKeever was his grandson and was 5 years of age. He was killed at the Victoria where he had gone with his brother Thomas who was taken out of the crush and his life was restored. The father of the deceased was sea-going fireman.

Hugh Blyth Allan, 13 North Bridge Street, surgeon, identified the bodies of Margaret Cook Allan, 7 years of age, and Michael Allan, 5 years of age, his daughter and son.

John Curry, blacksmith, 91 Back Whitburn Street, said the deceased John Curry was his son, and was 8 years of age. He had gone with his brother Charles, 6 years of age, and his cousin George Wallet 6 years of age.

Matthew Phillipson, foreman riveter, 12 Dame Dorothy Sweet, said Emerson Phillipson was his son, and was 11 years of age.

Charles Gilles, shipwright, 27 Dame Dorothy Street, identified John Robertson Gilles, five years age, as his son. The deceased was, with his two brothers and a cousin. Willen, labourer, residing at Zetland Street, said John Henry Willen was his son 11 years of age. He was the entertainment with his sister Sarah, eight years of age. Robert Tyndale Dodds, pilot, 73 Victor Street, said Charles Foster Dodds was his son, and was six years of age. He was at the entertainment with his brother, Robert Dodds nine years.

John Dring, adjuster, 32 Dock Street East, said John Robert Dring was his son, and was 11 years of age. The deceased went the hall with his cousin, Charles Dring. Robert Dring, foreman shipwright, residing at 61 Roker Avenue, said Charles eight years of age, was his son.

Thomas Jefferson, plater, 27 Gosforth Street, identified Thomas Jefferson, nine years of age, as his son, he went with his cousin and another boy.

Wm. Bell, riveter, 4 Bright Street, said William George Bell was his son, and was eight years of age. He went with three boys, named Wm. Peary, Andrew Wright, and Emerson Philipson. (They all lost their lives.)

Thomas Peary, boiler riveter, 4 Bright Street, identified William. Peary, nine years age, as his son.

Andrew Wright, driller, 5 Bright Street, said Andrew Wright, seven years age, was his son.

Thomas Kelty driller, 17 Dock Street East, said William Kelty, 10 years of age, was his son. The deceased had gone, with his sister Mary Ann.

Henry Watson, brickwork's manager, 136 Wayman Street, said Amy Lancaster Watson, 13 years of age, Robert Hollings Watson, 12 years of age, and Annie Emily Hollings Watson, 10 years of age, were his sisters and brother.

Mary Welsh, widow, said Ruth Athey, 11 years of age, and Jana Athey, 9 years of age, were the children of her nephew, who resided at 125 Wayman Street.

Robert Rowell, holder-up, Gladstone Street, said Elizabeth Rowell, 7 years of age, was his daughter, went with her three sisters.

William Davison, Cartwright, 11 High Street East, said Davison was six years of age, and his grand daughter.

Ann Harrison said she was the wife of John Harrison, seagoing engineer. Thomas Harrison was her son, and was seven years of age.

John George Venus, draper, 89 Ellington Street said John George Thomas Venus was his son, and was seven years of age.

John Gibson, 16 Tower Street, engine fitter, said John George Gibson, 11 years of age, was his son.

William Weighill, Vine Cottage, Park Road, identified William Robson Weighill, 8 years of age, his cousin. The deceased was a son of Thomas Weighill, painter.

William Kirby, striker, Trinity Place, identified Alfred Edward Kirby, 10 years of age, son of William Kirby a mariner, 19 D'Arcy Terrace.

John Spence, 30 Howick Street, Monkwearmouth boat builder, identified the body Joseph Spence, 10 year of age, lying in the Infirmary, as his son. The deceased was killed on Saturday by the crush.

Thomas Russell, 29 Lawrence Street, painter, that Mary Russell, 5 years of was his daughter. She went the Victoria hall with other two children.

Snaith, 7 East Street, butcher, said George Snaith, 8 years of age, was his son.

Julius Solomon, 43 Henry Street, glazier, identified Dinah Solomon, 9 years of age, as his daughter.

Graham, 37 New Gray Street, mariner, said Thomas, 7 years of age, was his son. George Stewart, 1 Sans close seaman, identified William Simpson 6 year's age, the son of S Simpson deceased. Witness picked the boy up dead at the Victoria Hall. Eliza Whitestore, Workhouse Gate, identified John Edward Dixon, aged 6 years, son of Leonard Charles Dixon, tailor, living 6 Howick Street.

Richard Evans of 16 Thompson Street, identified George Evans 10 and Charles Evans 8 as his brothers, are lying dead at 16 Thompson Street.

John Hutchinson, 72 Hendon Road, fruitier, identified Laura Vike Hutchinson, his daughter, 6 years and 8 months. Was dead when picked up on Saturday night. Margaret Garland, Back Norman Street, New Hendon, identified Margaret Annie Turnbull, 9 years of age, daughter of Henry Turnbull, helper shipyard. She was dead got out. She also identified Margaret Thompson, 6 years, and daughter of Richard Thompson, mason, living at 26 Norman Street.

Thomas Elliott, 19 Burleigh Street, Sunderland, a seaman, identified James Oliver Elliott aged 8 and Alice Watt Elliott, 10 and years of age, who were got out dead. John Robertson, 61 High Street, confectioner, identified Ann Robertson and Ethel Robertson, 10 years and 9 months and 7 years and two months old respectively, his daughters. When got out they were dead.

John Potts Hylton, 41 Emma Street, Hendon, identified John Potts Hylton, his son, aged 6, got out dead.

Ellen Wise 56 Moor Street identified John James Wise, 10 years, son of John Wise, living at Moor Street, a mariner.

Thomas Davison, 104 High Street East, shipwright, identified John Clarke Davison, 6 years and 5 months old, his son.

Martin Hutchinson Davison, 73 Tweed Street, boat builder, identified his son, named Martin Hutchinson, 8 years of age.

William Snaith, 57 Fowler Terrace, Hendon, identified Elizabeth Snaith, his child, 8 years got out dead.

James Scott, 23 Vine Street, labourer, identified James Henry Scott, 9 years of age, and Thomas William Scott, 7 years, his son; got out dead—one at the Victoria Hall, and the other laying in the Palatine Hotel.

Benjamin Dykstra, police officer, Identified Ada Topping aged 11 got out dead; also identified Norah Topping, aged 6 years and 3 months, as the daughters of John Topping a Coal fitter 47 Emma Street.

Matthew McCann of Silver Street, a labourer identified Catherine McCann, his daughter, 8 years old.

Peter Conlin, of 48 Burleigh Street, a labourer, identified Margaret Jane Conlin, 10 years old, his daughter, who was got out dead.

George Hopper Tomlinson, of 2 Bridge Street, auctioneer, identified Annie May age 4 years, his granddaughter, and daughter of Robert Hopper Tomlinson, auctioneer's clerk.

Peter Ahlgren, Parade, New Henden, identified Charles John Ahlgren, his son, 8 years of age.

Lawrence, of 1 Addison Street, Hendon solicitor's clerk, identified Isabel Lawrence. Joan George Crouch Lawrence, 7 and 5 years of age, his children.

John Ramsay, 30 Covent Garden Street, tailor, identified Robert Ramsay, his son, 11 years old got out dead.

John Bell, Pemberton Street, Bishopwearmouth, mason, identified James Bell, his son, 6 years of age; got out dead.

John Vowell, 5 Norfolk Street, a copper plater, identified his sisters, Grace Newton Vowell, 8years, and Lily Vowell, 4 years, daughters of David Vowell, coppersmith. George Kemp, 24 Henry Street East, dock trimmer, identified his son, William Kemp 7.

Thomas Bailey, 39 East Street, Bishopwearmouth, shipwright, identified Thomas Bailey, his son, 8; got out dead.

B. Rackstraw, of11 Burleigh Street, identified John Thomas Proudfoot, 8 years of age. of Ann Proudfoot, now Ann Webster, wife of William Webster, labourer; got out dead.

Ann Adams, 5 Parade, identified Margaret Grey Adams, daughter of Jesse Adams, 11 years of age, whom she picked up dead in the hall.

William Howard, 3 Pemberton Street, Bishopwearmouth, sailor, identified John Howard, 6 years as his son.

Joseph Brown, 16 D'Arcy Street, waterman, identified Margaret Ellen Brown, 12 years, his daughter; dead when got out.

William Pescod, 21 Burleigh Street, striker, identified William Henry Pescod, aged 10 years and 3 months, his son got out dead; and Mary Eleanor Pescod, 8 years and 3 months, his daughter got out dead. (In 1888 the family would have a daughter who they named after Mary Eleanor. In fact their son Robert would marry a girl called Mary Eleanor.)

Thomas Swinburne Ritson, Mordey Street, shipwright, identified Thomas Curry Ritson, 7 years and 8 mouths, his son.

Edward Liddle, of 34 Burlington Road, ship wright, identified Edward Liddle, his son, 8 years of age: got out dead.

Thomas Graham, Bramwell Street, identified Frederick William Graham, his son, aged 11 years and 8 months.

John Wilkinson, 7 Addison Street East, guard, identified his son, Robert Wilkinson, 7 years, got out dead.

James Jeffrey, 15 Covent Garden, identified Margaret Orrock, 12 years of age, daughter of John Orrock, plumber, deceased when got out was dead.

Michael Robson, 14 Tyne Street, identified Eleanor Robson, his daughter, aged 6 years and 4 months.

Mary Hindmarch, wife of John identified Barbara Blakey, aged 10years ago, daughter of William Blakey, No. 1 Vane Terrace, New Henden.

John Meek, labourer, Villiers Street identified James Meek, his son, 8 years; got out dead.

Joseph Kirton, Carr's Yard, Ball Street, Sunderland, waterman, identified Elizabeth Kirton, aged 9 years, his daughter, who was picked out, by him, dead.

James Carr, 13 Trinity Place, identified Charles Henry Kerr, his .son, 8 years old.

John Hogg, 4 Addison Street East, filter, Identified Robert Hogg, 8 years.

George Simey, fitter, of 55 Silver Street, identified Abraham Smith Simey, 8 son of James Simey, shipwright, 55 Silver Street.

Mary Jane Roper 17 of 12 East Cross Street identified her sister Margaret Roper, 8 years, and daughter of Isabella Roper, widow.

Barker Ramsay Cogdon, 21 Flag Lane, waterman, identified Barker Ramsay 8 years of age, his son, got out just alive, but could not fetch him 'about.'

William Beall, 32 Ford Street, Bishopwearmouth, fitter, identified James Wm. Beall, 8 years and 3 months, his son. The child died immediately he was got out.

Davison Bell, 25 Norman Street, jeweller, identified Isabella Bell, his daughter, 7 years and nine months; got out dead.

Mary Ann Swinney, wife of Tobias Swinney, labourer, identified John Thomas Swinney, aged 7 years.

Andrew Booth, 31 Peacock Street, identified Robert William Booth, 9 years, son of Thomas Booth, shipwright, got out alive, but died near the hall.

Thomas Taylor, riveter, Coatsworth Street, identified John James Taylor, aged 9 years, his son, and Thomas Toward, 9 years age, son of Agnes Toward (Thomas Taylor identified Toward because he worked with the boy's grandfather and they lived in the same street. Some sources list him as being his son.)

Dixon Morris, Glebe Cleft Villas, Chester Road, metal broker, identified Emily Morris, his daughter, aged 7.

Robert Chandler, of Millfield, holder up, identified Thomas Henry Chandler, 10 years of age, and his son and also identified Jane Chandler, 6 years of age, his daughter.

Richard Hughes Iron shipyard worker 1 Swinbank Street, identified his son, Thomas Edward Hughes, aged 5 years.

Anthony Thompson, 31 Palmer Street, shipwright, identified Mary Ann Thompson, 11 his daughter, and Margaret Thompson, aged 3 years 7 months.

Thomas Duncan, William Street, Millfield, identified Mary Ann Duncan, daughter, 11years old, got out dead.

George Paley, 15 Garden Place, pattern maker, identified Edward Paley, 6 years of age, his son.

Jane Scrafton, 6 Handel Street, wife of James Scrafton, boiler smith, identified Eugene Scrafton, aged 8 years.

Thomas Longstaff, Coatsworth Street, mariner, identified William Sinclair Longstaff, 6 years age last birthday, his son, who was got out dead.

Robert Sewell, 23 Lime Street, trimmer, identified Mary Ann Ayre, aged 8, daughter of Tamer Ayre, trimmer, of 15 Deptford Road.

George Fenwick, 43 High Street, greengrocer, identified Cuthbert Fenwick 6 years and 8 months old, as his son.

William Rutherford, outfitter, John Candlish Road, identified William Rutherford, aged 7 years and 11 months, his son. When got out was alive and lived for an hour and half afterwards in Rutland Street, where he had been taken on his way to his home.

James Kirton, 4 Clanny Street, identified Alfred David Kirton, aged 5, and James Frederick, 9, as his sons.

John William Brodie, commission agent, 3 Buxton Terrace, identified John Brodie, 8 years of age, brought out dead from the hall.

Jonathan Dunn, Colliery Row, Dun Cow Street, stock taker in rolling mills, identified Thomas Harper Dunn, 9 years, his son got out dead

John Hughes, tailor, living 5, Clanny-Street, Bishopwearmouth, identified the body of Thomas Hughes (7) his son.

Thomas Rochester Fox. 11 Chester Terrace North, mariner, identified William Rochester Fox (9).

Philip Maddison, 39, Somerford place, upholsterer and cabinetmaker, identified Frederick Maddison and Sarah Kennedy Maddison (5). The bodies are laying at 10 Kingsley-Street, also identified George Prior (12) of 10 Kingsley street son of George Prior, forgeman.

William Patchet, 20 Lisburn terrace. Diamond Hall, labourer, identified Mary Patchet his daughter.

John Patterson, 6, Matlock-street, Bishopwearmouth, porter, identified his son. Alfred.

Peter Fairgrieve, 17, Brougham-street, seaman, identified James (10) and Peter (7) Fairgrieve, his sons.

Jane Moore, 46, Wear-street, Bishopwearmouth, identified John Fenwick (8), son of Charles Fenwick, coal trimmer.

George. Brown, 13, Lisburn-terrace, Diamond Hall, boiler smith, identified Margaret Jane Brown (4) as his daughter.

William Downey, 5, Back Sussex-street, labourer, identified his daughter, Mary Downey, aged 7. Deceased was dead at the Infirmary on Saturday night about seven o'clock.

Susanna Wilson, wife John Wilson, joiner, identified Mary Ann Redman (14), daughter of David Redman, painter, deceased. She died whilst being transported to the Infirmary.

(Susanna was the sister of David)

The last six bodies yet to be identified were removed to the police station where they were placed in the lower cells. Five of the children were identified during the early hours of the morning. William Briggs aged 9 of 19 Blandford Street became the last child to be identified at 6 am by his Father, (reported as a cab proprietor but in the 1881 he is listed as a Cattle feed manufacturer). His brother Newrick aged 4 had died earlier in the crush.

How harsh are the 'words got out dead'

Occupations of the parents.

Adjuster
Arcade caretaker
Auctioneer
Boat builder(s)
Baker(s)
Basket Maker
Blacksmith
Boiler riveter (s)
Boilermaker (s)
Bottle blower
Brickwork manager.
Cab proprietor
Cartmen
Cartwright (s)
Chain striker
Coal Miner
Coal teamer (looked after horses)
Commercial Traveller
Commission Agent
Confectioner
Coppersmith
Doctor
Engine Fitter(s)
Engineer of Steamer
Engine Model Maker
Fruitier
Furniture Dealer
Glazier
Glass Works Manager

Holder Up	Railway engine driver
Iron Furnace man	River Pilot
Jeweller	Rolling Mills Stock
Labourer (s)	Sail maker
Mason (s)	Seamen /Mariner(s)
Miller(s)	Shipwrights
Outfitter	Shipyard Plater(s)
Painter	Shop man Clothier
Pattern Maker	Solicitors General clerk
Pawnbroker	Steam ship Inspector
Plane Maker	Surgeon
Plumber	Tailor
Police Officer	Tiler
Porter	Tinsmith
Provision Dealer	Waterman
	Wood carver

Women's occupations are lacking in the early Census as they were undervalued and thought not worthy to include. They were usually listed as Engine fitter's wife etc. The occasional dressmaker, domestic duties and cleaner were stated but in a general way. Charwoman would appear more often in 1901 census. There is no doubt that a huge number of women worked, despite having large families, to help with the family budget. This would be evident in families whose mother had lost her husband through death or the woman had been deserted. In some cases the husband would not want to confirm to the census, that his wife had to work to subsidies his wages. The list of the bereaved's occupations reveals that the majority of the dead children came from the working class. No doubt influenced in some ways by the cheaper admission price in the gallery. The occupations above are taken from the Census for 1881 plus the report from The Sunderland Echo.

Agnes Greig aged 5 was the last child to fall asleep. She had attended Victoria hall and was not involved with the crush but witnessed the aftermath with her sister.

An inquest was held at the Old Fellow Arms on her death on the Friday after the tragedy

Jane Greig, widow of Jonathan Greig, blacksmith, said that the deceased was her daughter. She was fine at school all the week_ until Sunday, and seemed to be weary and fretting about the children lost at the Victoria Hall. She and her sister got upset at seeing the other children being carried out. She was nervous at night, and cried out in her sleep. Friday morning she just lay across her bed. She wouldn't have any breakfast, and during the day she was dozing in and out. She was murmuring the prayers that the teachers had taught them to say about the little ones. About four o'clock her mother asked her to take a little tea, but she refused so her mother lay with her on the couch for minute or two. Then as the mother rose to leave her she discovered that she was dead. No marks or bruises could be found. Her sister Ada said she had fallen down on the flags in the hall, but was not in the crush at the bottom of the stairs.

Dr Drinkwater deposed that he was called little before five, Friday afternoon. The body was quite warm, and she had evidently just died. There were bruises to be seen, but the entire surface was very much congested. He rather suspected poisoning, but there had been neither diarrhoea nor vomiting.

The Coroner: Would you say it was death from poison?

Drinkwater: No, I would not say that. It's something, which has interfered with the action of the heart to cause congestion of

the veins of the body. Had not been syncope, or the surface the body would have been very pale. Might been some form of brain disease brought on by fright.

The Coroner: Has she had medicine of any kind?

Mrs Greig: No she did not require any.

Dr Drinkwater: Have you not given her anything to make her sleep or rest?

Just tea.

The Coroner: you say, doctor, that there is a suggestion of this child having been poisoned; it is our duty to order a post-mortem examination. If she has died from poison, we will have to ascertain who poisoned her.

It was later reported that the Coroner's inquest found that the death of Agnes Greig had resulted from 'a fatal convulsion arising from a shock to the nervous system in consequence of the Victoria hall crush.

Researchers are reluctant to include her in the list of fatalities but to me, you must.

Another mystery, which surrounds Victoria hall deaths, was the strange case of the Atkinson children. It appears that two children, named Mary Jane and Frederick Atkinson, aged respectively eight years and five years, had come to Sunderland on a visit to their sick grandmother, their grandfather was a mariner and away at sea. As a little treat they were allowed to go to the entertainment at the Victoria Hall. After the show they were caught up with the crush on the stairs. Here, like so many others, they received bruises about the head, but the bruises were not considered to be serious, plasters being placed upon them by the doctors. They returned home to their Grandmothers house where their mother and her brother who had accompanied them to Sunderland were waiting. The same evening, they returned to their home in South Shields. On the train it was noticed that they seemed to be drowsy, and were short tempered if anyone tried to talk to them. The doctor was consequently called in when they reached home, but they gradually deteriorated and both died within two hours of each other on Monday morning. The father, who was a sailor, was at sea, and of course knew nothing of the loss of his two children.

This story was repeated in many newspapers, it has such fine detail it is worth considering but because there was no known burial site the story was dismissed as untrue. I have been told that Mary Jane could be buried in South Shields but I have no knowledge of Frederick, they are not usually listed in the dead.

Another death attributed to the disaster was William Robinson who was the son of the publican who ran The Argo Frigate in West Wear Street. He worked in the pub as a barman. On hearing about the calamity at Victoria Hall he went there as several of 'his locals' had children attending the show. He helped with the removal of children of his friends and was completely *overcome with sadness* He returned to the public house and felt unwell. He had the feeling that *'he was paralysed and had congestion of the lungs.'* It was reported that he was a fit man and was an expert swimmer but unfortunately he died the next day, another possible casualty of the disaster.

The victims of the disaster comprised 70 girls and 116 boys. (Disputed)

The following shows the numbers and ages of the children

Ages	14	13	12	11	10	9	8	7	6	5	4	3
Victims	1	1	6	13	26	24	37	37	19	15	5	2

If we study the table above it would seem that Berwick was wrong in thinking that the girl he pulled from the crush was '16 or 17' he also stated that she belonged to the family that had suffered three deaths, Only the Watson family lost 3 children so it could have been Amy Hollings Watson who was 13. Another possibility is that it`s poor Annie Redman who lived in 4 Booth Street and acted as a servant / nurse for the family. Two children died from this address so Berwick could have been misled into thinking they were all from the same family.

The two three year olds who died were

Dorothy Buglass of 21Thornton Place who died in the arms of her sister Ann.

Margaret Thompson who died with her sister **Mary Ann** aged 11 of 31 Palmer Street. They were found locked together.

The eldest was **Mary Anne Redman** of 4 Booth Street where on the censor for 1881 she was listed as a servant. I believe when she died she was an orphan.

The streets, which contained the most children killed, were Gilsland Street, Clanny Street, Wayman Street and Burleigh Street.

An appeal was made to *'those who has recently been in deep mourning could send a box of black dresses, crape bonnets, etc., which they do not require, if they would likely to prove useful to any of the sorrowing mothers and if any are in sufficiently poor circumstances to accept such help.'*

If you don't remember their names they will die

❧❧❧

John Taylor

Chapter 8
The Funerals

Sunderland and surrounding areas turned out in force to pay respects to the children as they were brought by their grief stricken parents, relations and friends to their last resting-places. The burials took place in three different sites. Bishopwearmouth, Sunderland and Mere Knolls the cemeteries appointed for the several districts. It was a general idea that the day should be partially observed as a holiday, and that blinds should be drawn as a mark of respect to the memory of the deceased. At most of the shipyards and engine shops the men ceased work at breakfast-time, the remainder, as well as many other places of business, and schools were closed for the day at noon. A consequence of this cessation of labour was that the streets were thronged with spectators during the afternoon. Sympathetic crowds collected in the thoroughfares leading to the different cemeteries to see the funeral processions pass along. It was firstly suggested by the council that all the interments should take place in one cemetery. The parents disagreed preferring to bury their children in the districts where they reside and where other members of the family were interred. Following a discussion it was agreed that the parent's plan should be followed resulting in a few being buried outside the boundaries of Sunderland. The council stated.

Sad scenes have been only too frequent during the past few days, and there were enough to make the heart bleed without the spectacle of a public funeral. .

What follows is a digested account of some of the funerals carried out at the three cemeteries.

At noon on the 19th of June, the interments in **The Bishopwearmouth Cemetery,** Chester-road, commenced. A local reporter described the scene

A soft gentle breeze was blowing at the time, the sky was cloudy, and there was occasional shower of rain. Inside the cemetery grounds the flowers and shrubs looked bright and cheerful, and the lovely foliage and pretty flowers inspired anything but a feeling of gloom, and made it difficult to imagine that in a couple of hours many of the little unfortunates were here to be committed to the tomb. The central terrace from Hylton-road to Chester-road is fringed by beautiful flowers exquisite bloom, looking all the better for the recent rain. Behind them the deep fringe of trees helped to give the visitor an idea that this could not possibly be the land of the dead. I wandered round some of the principal pathways, and looked at the numerous headstones, large and small, surrounded by shrubs, and looking down on beds of flowers. Some men were busily working here and there, preparing for the interments, which were so soon to take place.

The entire route to the burial ground was lined with thousands of people including tradesmen, shopkeepers, and school children. Most families in the districts through which the funerals passed either drew their window blinds or half closed their shutters. The gates of the cemetery were guarded by a strong force of the county constabulary, who allowed only a few people to be admitted, in addition to the sorrowing relatives of the deceased children. Many relatives and friends of the deceased were refused entry, which was upsetting for those who had travelled a great distance to pay their respects. On the consecrated side of the ground thirty graves had been dug, situated a little to the southeast of the church. They were eight feet long and about twenty inches in breadth, separated by a soil partition nine inches thick. In each of the graves two children were buried, the coffins being placed end to end-making sixty the number to be interred in this spot. Four graves had been prepared in the church ground for private burials. These were situated at about 200 yards north of the general burying place for the children, and midway between the Established and Dissenting chapels. In the unconsecrated portion of the cemetery, a hundred yards north- east of the chapel was the children's free ground, where there had been twenty long graves in which to bury forty children. A little to the west there are six private graves. The first burial to take place was Elizabeth Wanless. A Laburnham tree with branches of wilting yellow blossom fell over the small grave of Elizabeth, shading her and the surrounding sorrow.

The scenes at the graves were of a very affecting character. While the last words were being read over Elizabeth the child of Mr Wanless, who held in his hand two wreaths of flowers, could not control his feelings. He leaned forward and looked into the grave, and, utterly overcome, his grief found vent in a flood of tears that rolled down his cheeks. At times he couldn't control himself.

Two boys, one Thomas H. Crishop, son of the undertaker and an apprentice named James Lowry carried the coffin containing the body of Louise Paxton. Mrs. Paxton's reaction at the grave was heartrending.

The Day the Children Fell Asleep

Mrs. Paxton mother of Louise Isabella was disconsolate. She sobbed as if her heart would break, and was led away from the side of the grave crying, 'I canna leave my bairn! I canna leave my bairn!'

The funeral that aroused most interest was that of the four children, the sons and daughters, of Mr and Mrs., Mills of Ann Street. We can only imagine what it is like to bury four of your children on the same day. The whole street was in mourning, over the bright young lives, that the neighbours viewed each day but were no longer there. The door that was opened only a few days earlier to release excited children into the sunshine now on a cloudy dank day opened on the parents Richard and Margaret Mills. They had to be physically supported by relations, unaware of the surrounding grief of others, just lost in their own. The local paper described the scene

Yesterday it was reported that Mrs. Mills was dead, but we are glad to say that further enquiry showed that the statement was unfounded. As the cortege passed through the town the profoundest sympathy was expressed for the mother in a bereavement that had well nigh cost her reason, if not her life. The four coffins were contained in a hearse, which, having glass sides enabled all to see the beautiful wreaths of flowers, which had been placed upon them by loving friends. The four children were interred in two graves, purchased by Mr Mills in the Dissenting ground, and the coffins were laid side by side. When the graves were filled up, a wreath of white flowers was placed on top. The two girls shared one plot, as did their two brothers.

At the interment of Charles Henry Lane 10 and his brother James William 6 there were about 100 members of the Salvation Army standing to attention, as the two boys had been *'little soldiers of the army.'* The detachment were under the command of Captain Reed, and they sang very impressively, the hymn *'One sweetly solemn thought'* which includes the lines *'I am nearer home today than I have ever been before.'*

The funeral of Elizabeth Halliman aged 8 the daughter of John and Mary Ann who would later have engraved on her gravestone the line *In the midst of life we are in death.* And despite the grief the parents must have been suffering, devoted an added line to the stone *Thank thee O Lord for the children saved.*

The local M.P. wrote

Never shall I forget the melancholy and impressive scenes that I beheld yesterday I drove through the long lines and dense masses of our people on my way to the cemeteries. Gloom seemed to hang over every face, at once telling how deeply one and all felt and mourned over the appalling calamity with which we have been afflicted The cemeteries procession succeeded procession, each bearing gracefully, in neat and elegant caskets adorned with simple garlands, to its last resting-place, one of those lifeless but angelic forms which but as yesterday was "all joyous as the noon-day sun" with life, but now, alas! Conclusion, allow me to say how much I sympathise with the bereaved parents and relatives, earnestly hoping that one and all may be upheld and succored by that Divine hand which alone can help both now and hereafter.

The funerals came slowly during the day, but this was owing to the difficulty in getting enough vehicles, plus the crowds of onlookers filling the small streets. In several instances, where the ages of the deceased ranged from three to six years, young people with slings of white drapery carried the coffins to the graves. The scenes must have been compelling to watch, yet heartbreaking to experience

MERE KNOLLS. Cemetery is situated in a valley between Fulwell and Whitburn, and chiefly used for the interment of those who died in the Monkwearmouth portion of the borough. The graves were in four different parts of the ground. Thirty-one of the children who lost their lives in the Victoria Hall calamity would eventually be buried there. A number of men were employed during the night preparing the graves, and as they were finished, tickets bearing the names of the children to be buried in them, were placed beside them in order to prevent any confusion. The men stood aside with heads bowed and their caps taken from their heads as the families arrived. To each child were given a separate grave, except in cases where burials took place in what is known as the purchase ground. In one case a boy and two girls from the Watson family were placed in one resting-place. Of the twenty-three interments, twelve took place in the unconsecrated ground in unpurchased graves, eight in family burial grounds, one in consecrated purchase ground, and two in consecrated common ground. It was arranged that the interments should take place at any time convenient to the family and friends of the deceased. The burial service could be heard in the cemetery at any time from ten in the morning until six in the evening. Most of the streets of Monkwearmouth seemed to have either a hearse or mourning coaches in them during some part of the day. The community seemed to have entirely devoted the day to taking part in the solemn rites. In front of each house, the inmates of which were preparing to take their lost ones to the grave, a crowd assembled and silently watched the proceedings. Following the hearse in most cases were children who a few days earlier had played with their deceased school friends who stood holding hands with them in a playground, or next to them over a desk improving their handwriting.

The children buried at this cemetery included three children of the Watson family of 135 Wayman Street. Amy Lancaster 13, Annie Emily 10 and their brother Robert 12. Their bodies were encased in coffins of light coloured wood with silver-gilt mountings, and were carried direct to the side of the large grave. The brother and sister of the deceased, and other relatives and friends were present. A group captured in despair, not knowing how to console each other, the children's peers in bewilderment at their loss.

A local reporter portrayed the scene

They were very much affected, and as the service proceeded, the grief of the parents wasn't to be restrained. As the coffins were lowered, Mrs. Watson, who watched the priest with intense earnestness, exclaimed with much emotion, 'Put them in canny, oh, dear me. Put them in canny'

An emotional Mr McGonagall said over the graves.

It is our melancholy duty to take part this morning in one of the saddest rites that has ever been my lot to perform. I can scarcely trust myself to say even a few sentences,

He quoted from Thessalonians 4: 13 *'we sorrow not man without hope without which he added we might stand here silent. It is in the spirit of this hope that I would point you, my sorrowing friends, to the one true hope, the only comfort. To their one friend, their only comforter let them look away out of this life up to him who had taken those little ones away.*

During the delivery of this address Mr and Mrs. Watson and family '*wept bitterly.*'

Sunderland Cemetery.

Throughout the day scenes of the '*most heartrending description occurred*, and the terrible extent to which the disaster had reached was shown in a most realistic manner by there being at one time as many as three or four coffins waiting outside the little church while part of the burial-service was being conducted inside, and at the same moment another child was being lowered into its place of interment. The tolling of the chapel bell was almost incessant throughout the afternoon and rang in the mourner's ears all night.

The men working in this cemetery had been working steadfastly to prepare the graves. Twenty of them were dug close together in a prominent plot on the West side of the cemetery. They were arranged in three parallel rows, and so planned out as to leave at the far side a small site on which to erect a memorial of the event, if it should be desired to do so. The remaining eight graves were situated in various parts of the purchase space and lease- hold ground. The first funeral that took place at this cemetery was that of Andrew Coupland, I1 years of age, living at 40, Queen Street, it reached the gates at half-past eleven. At that time there were very few people in the cemetery around the grave, just the parents and friends of the deceased. Towards the afternoon numbers of spectators took up positions on the Ryhope Road to witness the melancholy processions as they passed along. Such was the crush around the entrance to the burial ground that the superintendent found it necessary to communicate with Sergeant Clark, of Ryhope, for assistance,

That officer with a number of constables arrived shortly. There would then be some 2,000 or 3,000 persons on the road, many of whom were anxious to gain admission to the cemetery, and it was only by dint of great exertions on the part of the officers that perfect order was kept.

James Hayhurst 7 belonged to the Rectory Park School and as a mark of respect the children belonging to his class, their teacher H. G. Cray and a monitor named John McKenzie, accompanied his remains to the grave. Each of the boys carried a bouquet, and at the end of the service they approached the grave two by two and laid the flowers upon the coffin. They passed Margaret Hayhurst with her eight remaining children clinging to her and their father. The five sisters had attended the show with James but had escaped the crush. Their Mother would soon be pregnant again and would give birth to twins in 1884. She would die in 1907 and would be buried close to James. The twins would be called Ethel and Michael James and when Michael married he named his first daughter Ethel.

The Toppin sisters Ada and Nora from Emma Street were buried, their grief stricken parents supported by workmates from the pit where Mr Toppin was employed as a trimmer.

The brother and sister James 10 and Alice Elliott 8 from Burleigh Street were interred, watched by their father, who had returned from sea to be present.

Thomas Fleming and James Scott, half brothers from Vine Street were buried together at the request of their parents.

The next to arrive was that of Charles Kerr, eight years of age, who resided at Trinity Place. Belonging to a Catholic family, the service was read in the house, so that beyond the burial there was no ceremony around the grave. A long interval elapsed before the next funeral, which did not arrive at the cemetery till after six o'clock. It was that of two sisters, named Ann Pattison Robertson, ten years of age, and Ethel Robertson, seven years

The Day the Children Fell Asleep

of age who were interred in the purchase space of the cemetery. A long cortege followed the hearse, including a considerable number of children from the Tatham-Street Sunday School, of which the deceased were members. (It was reported that thirty members of this Sunday school perished but it is difficult to confirm this) This ceremony completed the unfortunate burials for the day at Sunderland Cemetery.

At Sunderland Cemetery on the second day, the interment of the children started at noon, when the body of Robert Ramsey, aged 11years, of Convent Garden Street was committed to the earth. There were few persons besides the immediate relatives and a number of schoolfellows of the deceased around the grave while the Rev. R. Waters read the solemn service. Wreaths and bunches of flowers were laid on the coffin before it was lowered into the grave. Selenium ferns had also arrived and were laid on the large plot where most of the children were buried. The burials did not stop until after seven o'clock

The town's public days of grief came to an end on 21st June 1883

This is a list of the believed dead children and where, when known, their resting place. Information has been collected from Genuki.org Sunderland,Yolasite.com. The Victoria Hall Disaster by Albert Anderson. The Durham Mining Museum (disasters.) Plus research by the author.

1	Adams	Margaret Gray	10	5 Parade	BW	19.06
2	Ahlgren	Charles John	8	23 Parade	BW	19.06
3	Allen	Michael	5	13 North Bridge Street	MK	20.06
4	Allen	Margaret Cook	7	13 North Bridge Street	MK	20.06
5	Anderson	George Frederick	7	24 Brougham Street	BW	20.06

6	Athey	Jane	9	125 Wayman Street	MK	19.06
7	Athey	Ruth	11	125 Wayman Street	MK	19.06
8	Ayre	Mary Ann.	8	15 Deptford Road	BW	20.06
9	Bailey	Thomas	8	39 East Street	BW	19.06
10	Beale	James William	8	32 Ford Street	BW	20.06
11	Bell	Isabella	7	25 Norman Street Hendon	BW	20.06
12	Bell	James	6	3 Pemberton Street	BW	20.06
13	Bell	William George	8	4 Bright Street	MK	19.06
14	Blakey	Barbara	10	7 Page Street	BW	19.06
15	Bland	William	10	66 Hedley Street	BW	20.06
16	Booth	Robert William	9	11 St Luke's Terrace		
17	Briggs	Newrick	4	19 Blandford Street	BW	20.06
18	Briggs	William James	9	19 Blandford Street	BW	20.06
19	Brodie	John William	8	3 Buxton Street	BW	19.06
20	Browell	Emily	9	8 Gilsland Street	Houghton Le Spring	21.06
21	Brown	Margaret Ellen	12	16 D'Arcy Street	Unknown	
22	Brown	Margaret Jane	4	13 Lisburn Terrace	BW	20.06
23	Buglass	Dorothy	3	21 Thornton Place	BW	20.06
24	Butler	Thomas	8	39 Thompson Street	BW	19.06
25	Carr	Charles Henry	8	13 Trinity Place	Unknown	
26	Chandler	Sarah Jane	7	17 Wilson Street Millfield	BW	19.06

27	Chandler	Thomas Henry	10	17 Wilson Street	BW	19.06
28	Cogdon	Barker Ramsey	8	21 Flag Lane	BW	20.06
29	Conlin	Margaret Jane	10	44 Burleigh Street	Unknown	
30	Coulson	George Henry	8	22 Watson Lane	BW	20.06
31	Coupland	Andrew		40 Queen Street	SD	19.06
32	Curry	John		91 Back Whitburn Street	MK	19.06
33	Davison	John Clark		104 High Street East	Unknown	
34	Davison	Martin Hutchinson		73 Tweed Street	BW	19.06
35	Davison	Rosannah		11 Thomas Street	MK	19.06
36	Dixon	Charles		Willow Pond Terrace	BW	20.06
37	Dixon	John Edward		6 Howick Street	Unknown	
38	Dodds	Charles	6	73 Victor Street	MK	20.06
39	Duncan	Mary Ann	11	13 William Street West	BW	20.06
40	Downey	Mary	7	1 Back Sussex Street	BW	20.06
41	Dring	Charles	8	61 Roker Avenue	MK	19.06
42	Dring	John Robert	11	32 Dock Street East	MK	19.06
43	Dumble	Elva	7	St Marks Road Hylton Street	BW	20.06
44	Dunn	Thomas Harper	9	11 Collier Row Dun Cow St	BW	19.06
45	Elliott	Alice Watt	8	19 Burleigh Street	SD	20.06

46	Elliott	James Oliver	10	19 Burleigh Street		20.06
47	Evans	Charles	9	16 Thompson Street	BW	20.06
48	Evans	John George	11	16 Thompson St	BW	20.06
49	Fairgrieve	James	10	17 Brougham Street	BW	19.06
50	Fairgrieve	Peter	7	17 Brougham Street	BW	19.06
51	Falley	Kate	9	7 Cornhill Road	Unknown	
52	Fenwick	Cuthbert Morrison	6	43 High Street West	BW	19.06
53	Fenwick	John	7	46 Wear Street	BW	20.06
54	Fleming	Thomas William	8	23 Vine Street	SD	20.06
55	Fox	George William	6	10 Gilsland Street	BW	20.06
56	Fox	Robert	9	10 Gilsland Street	BW	20.06
57	Fox	William Rochester	9	11 Chester Terrace North	BW	20.06
58	Gibson	John George	11	16 Tower Street	BW	19.06
59	Gillies	John Robertson	5	27 Dame Dorothy Street	MK	19.06
60	Graham	Frederick William	11	2 Bramwell Street Hendon	BW	20.06
61	Graham	Thomas	7	37 New Grey Street	SD	20.06
62	Greener	Thomas John	7	89 Eglinton Street	Unknown	
63	Grey	Robert Henry	7	21 Hawthorn Street	BW	20.06
64	Hall	Mary Ann	8	15 Deptford Road	Unknown	
65	Hall	Thomas	8	23 Alexandra Terrace	BW	20.06

66	Halliman	Elizabeth	8	12 Grey's Buildings	BW	19.06
67	Harker	William	6	26 Tees st	BW	19.06
68	Harrison	Thomas Harrison	9	11 Abbs Street	MK	20.06
69	Hayhurst	James	7	2 High Street West	SD	20.06
70	Henderson	Cicely	11	3 Hopper Street	BW	20.06
71	Henderson	James	10	3 Hopper Street	BW	20.06
72	Henderson	Margaret Jane	9	3 Hopper street	BW	20.06
73	Henderson	Richard	7	6 Nicholson Street	BW	19.06
74	Hilton	John Potts	6	41 Emma Street	BW	20.06
75	Hines	Arthur W N	8	4 Booth Street	BW	20.06
76	Hines	Eveline	6	4 Booth Street	BW	20.06
77	Hogg	Robert Hall	8	4 Harrison Street East	BW	19.06
78	Howard	John	7	3 Pemberton Street	BW	20.06
79	Hughes	Thomas Edward	5	1 Swinbank Street	BW	19.06
80	Hughes	Thomas	7	5 Clanny Street	BW	19.06
81	Hutchinson	Laura Voke	6	72 Hendon Road	BW	20.06
82	Jefferson	Thomas	9	20 Gosforth Street	MK	19.06
83	Jewitt	Reginald	10	Foyle Street	BW	19.06
84	Johnson	William	11	4 Pickard Street Millfield	BW	19.06
85	Kelly	William	10	17 Dock Street East	MK	19.06
86	Kemp	Joseph	8	27 Flag Lane	BW	20.06

87	Kemp	William	7	24 Henry Street East	BW	20.06
88	Kerr	Charles	8	13 Trinity Place	BW	19.06
89	Kirby	Alfred Edward	10	19 D'Arcy Terrace	BW	20.06
90	Kirton	Alfred David	5	4 Clanny Street	SD	19.06
91	Kirton	James Fred	8	4 Clanny street	SD	20.06
92	Kirton	Elizabeth	9	1 Carr's yard	BW	19.06
93	Knox	George Bright	9	6 Brougham Street	BW	20.06
94	Lackenby	Johnson	4	50 Queen Street	BW	20.06
95	Lane	Charles Henry	10	2 Clanny Street	BW	20.06
96	Lane	James William	6	2 Clanny Street	BW	20.06
97	Lawrence	Isabella	7	1 Addison Street	BW	20.06
98	Lawrence	John George	5	1 Addison Street	BW	20.06
99	Liddle	Edward	8	34 Burlington Road	BW	20.06
100	Longstaff	William Sinclair	7	Coatsworth Street	BW	19.06
101	Maddison	Frederick	5	10 Kingsley Street	BW	19.06
102	Maddison	Sarah Kennedy	9	10 Kingsley Street	BW	19.06
103	Marley	John	5	7 Tees Street	BW	20.06
104	McCann	Catherine	8	31 Silver Street	SD	19.06
105	McConkie	Nellie	10	6 Christopher Street	BW	20.06
106	McKeever	John William	5	1 Society Lane	MK	20.06

107	Meek	James	8	30 Villiers Street	BW	20.06	
108	Metcalfe	Jane Alice	4	6 Catherine Street	BW	19.06	
109	Milburn	Hannah Isabel	9	Alderson Street	BW	20.06	
110	Miles	Charles	9	19 Catherine Street	BW	19.06	
111	Miller	Emily	9	3 Gilsland Street	Unknown		
112	Miller	William	8	34 Burlington Road	BW	20.06	
113	Mills	Alice Purchase	10	10 Ann Street	BW	19.06	
114	Mills	Elizabeth Ann	12	10 Ann Street	BW	19.06	
115	Mills	Frederick	8	10 Ann Street	BW	19.06	
116	Mills	Richard	6	10 Ann Street	BW	19.06	
117	Morris	Emily	7	17 Glebe Cleft Villas	Unknown		
118	Morrison	John	7	15 Richmond St	MK	20.06	
119	Muse	Mary Jane	6	17 Biss Street	BW	19.06	
120	Newton	Catherine	8	13 Carter Street	Unknown		
121	Nipper	George Stokel	9	11 Howick Square	MK	19.06	
122	Noble	John Walter	11	13 Winchester Terrace	Unknown		
123	Orrock	Margaret Annie	12	15 Covent Garden Street	Unknown		
124	Patchet	Mary	10	20 Lisburn Terrace	BW	19.06	
125	Paley	Edward	6	15 Garden Place	BW	19.06	
126	Patterson	Alfred	9	6 Matlock Street	Unknown		
127	Paxton	Louisa	8	65 Tower Street	BW	19.06	
128	Peace	Anna Marie	7	22 Stanley Street	BW	20.06	

129	Pearey	Thomas	9	4 Bright Street	MK	19.06
130	Pescod	Mary Eleanor	5	21 Burleigh Street	Unknown	
131	Pescod	William Henry	10	21 Burleigh Street	Unknown	
132	Phillipson	Emmerson	11	12 Dame Dorothy Street	MK	19.06
133	Pringle	Ann Milner	9	48 Southwick Road	MK	19.06
134	Pringle	Margaret Milner	7	48 Southwick Rd	MK	19.06
135	Prior	George	12	11 Burleigh Street	BW	20.06
136	Proudfoot	John Thomas	8	11 Burleigh Street	SD	20.06
137	Ramsay	Robert	11	36 Covent Garden Street	SD	20.06
138	Redman	Mary Ann	14	4 Booth Street Hylton Road	BW	20.06
139	Richmond	Catherine Middlemiss	7	15 Grey's Buildings	BW	19.06
140	Ritson	Thomas Terry	9	18 Mordey Street	BW	20.06
141	Robertson	Ann Patterson	10	61 High Street East	SD	19.06
142	Robertson	Ethel	7	61 High Street East	SD	19.06
143	Robson	Eleanor	6	14 Tyne Street	BW	20.06
144	Roper	Margaret	8	12 East Cross Street	BW	20.06
145	Rowell	Elizabeth	7	48 Gladstone Street	MK	20.06
146	Russell	Mary Helen	6	21 Lawrence Street	BW	20.06
147	Scott	James Henry	10	23 Vine Street	SD	20.06
148	Scrafton	Eugenie	8	6 Handel Street Millfield	BW	19.06

149	Shipley	Walter Gibson	10	Griffin's Buildings	MK	19.06
150	Simey	Abraham Smith	8	55 Silver Street	SD	20.06
151	Simpson	William	7	2 Sans Street	Unknown	
152	Sleightman	George	8	4 Hendon Street	Unknown	
153	Sleightman	William	6	4 Hendon Street	Unknown	
154	Smith	Caroline	6	43 North Street	BW	20.06
155	Snaith	Elizabeth	8	57 Fowler Terrace	BW	20.06
156	Snaith	George	8	7 East Street	BW	19.06
157	Solomon	Dinah	9	43 Henry Street	Unknown	
158	Spence	Joseph	10	30 Howick Street	MK	
159	Southern	Thomas	8	10 Catherine Street	BW	19.06
160	Swinney	John Thomas	6	George Street	Unknown	
161	Taylor	John James	8	13 Coatsworth Street	BW	19.06
162	Taylor	Andrew	4	13 Coatsworth street	BW	19.06
163	Thompson	Margaret	3	31 Palmer Street	BW	19.06
164	Thompson	Mary Ann	11	31 Palmer Street	BW	19.06
165	Thompson	Margaret Ann	11	25 Norman Street	BW	19.06
166	Tomlinson	Annie J	4	2 Bridge Street	BW	20.06
167	Topping	Ada Anne	11	47 Emma Street	SD	
168	Topping	Nora	6	47 Emma Street	SD	19.06
169	Toward	Thomas	9	13 Coatsworth St	BW	!9.06

170	Turnbull	Margaret	6	Norman St	BW	20.06
171	Venus	John George Thomas	7	89 Eglinton Street	MK	19.06
172	Vowell	Grace Newton	8	5½ Norfolk Street	BW	19.06
173	Vowell	Lilly	4	5½ Norfolk Street	BW	19.06
174	Wanless	Elizabeth	7	8 Dock Street	BW	19.06
175	Ward	Florence Edith	6	8 Back Charles Street	MK	19.06
176	Watson	Amy Hollings Lancaster	13	136 Wayman Street	MK	19.06
177	Watson	Annie Emily Hollings	10	136 Wayman Street	MK	19.06
178	Watson	Robert Hollings	12	136 Wayman Street	MK	19.06
179	Weighill	William Robson	8	Vine Cottage Park Road	BW	19.06
180	Wilkinson	Robert	7	7 Addison Street	BW	20.06
181	Willen	John Henry	11	37 Zetland Street	MK	20.06
182	Williamson	Robert	11	5 Johnson Street	BW	19.06
183	Wise	John James	10½	56 Moor Street	BW	19.06
184	Wright	Andrew	7	5 Bridge Street	MK	19.06
185	Wright	Mary	5	Willow Pond Inn	BW	20.06

I feel we should include Ava Greig who died a few days after the accident due to the shock of seeing the dead children.

I have been told that Mary Jane Atkinson could be buried in Westoe cemetery South Shields but I have no information on her brother Frederick.

William Browell, who was a frequent visitor to the Miller family house and appears in the 1881 census as a visitor, identified Emily Miller at the hall. Emily Browell also died in the disaster, which caused some confusion. Research shows they both should be included as they both were killed in the crush.

Thomas Toward whom in some lists is known as Taylor. In the 1881 census he is living with his Granddad on his maternal side under the name of Toward. His mother was the wife of Thomas Taylor who lived in the same street and 'recognised' young Thomas's body after the accident, I would imagine he was buried in B.W with the rest of his family.

John George Venus was buried with his infant brother who died of consumption shortly after the accident.

Mary Patchet sometimes listed as Paget.

Annie Marie Peace sometimes listed as Peice.

Louisa Paxton is listed in some publications as 14 Dunning Street although this could be the address of the Funeral Director.

Mr. F. Caws an architect from Sunderland, who designed the Elephant Tearooms and who would be called to the inquest for evidence on the safety of the hall, had attended the funerals. He spoke to a young boy at the gates of the cemetery. He asked the boy, who was 'just able to talk,' but had escaped after being somewhat crushed,

'Were the children crying out?'
The child replied 'Yes'
'What were they crying?'
'They were crying for their mams'

This map indicates the streets of grief from where the funerals started. Black spots indicate the deceased children from those streets.

Chapter 9
The Donations

The news of the tragedy quickly travelled around the world and donations started flooding in. It was soon realised that a committee would have to be formed to collate and collect the money. It would then be up to them to decide what was going to happen to the donations. The initial contributions were without a doubt for the parents who would be the most affected by the calamity. The first item to be dealt with should have been the cost of the funerals. The agenda of immediate actions, should not have been clouded by memorials, convalescent home and children's hospital all readily put forward by important 'town people.' The parents, the sufferers, the children, that is what instigated people to donate money. Instructions should have been sent to the funeral directors / undertakers to submit their bills. This would have released the parents from any additional concern. Unfortunately the importance of the calamity, which had received sympathetic responses from all over the country, was to overcome the committee with the sense of self-importance. They considered the money collected became their money to distribute as they thought fit. The attitude of 'we know best' and *'be grateful for the work we are doing for you'* prevailed.

A meeting of the newly formed committee to discuss the subscription fund was held and the Mayor, who presided, said *the meeting was called to decide in what form the fund should be applied.* He mentioned that already £1239 had been subscribed, and donations continued to flow unabated into the treasury. The Mayor suggested that they should divide this committee into several sub-committees, so to work *the affair more efficiently.* The first should be a Relief Committee, so as to relieve the immediate wants of those who were too poor to spare the money necessary for burials. The next should be a Committee of Sunday Schools to allow the children contributing a little sum each. The next was a Working Man's Committee, and he himself would like a Church and Chapel Committee. The Rev W. A. Walton proposed that the workmen the shipyards, factories, workshop, and benefit societies should be requested to send two members each to form a committee to work with the fund among the working classes. This was seconded by a Mr R. Cameron and carried. A motion from Mr. Rutherford to the effect that there should be two representatives of the Sunday School Union, two Church of England, .two Roman Catholics, and two from the day schools, was carried. He therefore moved the adoption of the resolution proposed Monday's meeting, viz, "First, that the fund applied to assist *the immediate wants of the bereaved parents; secondly, the erection of one or more memorials in the town, the amount not exceeding £250; and thirdly, that the surplus be expended in erecting and endowing a convalescent home mainly for children.* This was seconded by Alderman Storey, M.P., and carried unanimously.

This sounded like a plan, although the plethora of committees should have set off alarms bells. Why three or four should be thought necessary is hard to fathom. Along with the money, it would appear the committees would have to be collated. At first no workingmen were asked to join and more importantly any parents. Later, management from five large industrial companies was accepted on the board.

Not only money was promised, on the practical side, it was put forward that a message should be sent to the workhouse to start producing coffins suitable for children around 8 years old. I have found no proof of this idea bearing fruition. Music concerts were promised with the money raised being presented to the fund.

Madame Florence Grant has written a letter to the Mayor, stating that she will give a concert on the 12th July, at the Prince's Hall, Piccadilly, on behalf of the fund.

People offered vacations for mothers and children who had been affected by the incident. Queen Victoria had promised to send £50 and a wreath. She sent a telegram via Sir Henry Ponsonby on the Monday stating how upset she was at this awful calamity and that her heart bleeds for the many poor bereaved parents. She was also anxious *'to hear how the injured children were recovering.'*

The mayor added that he had a lady friend who was willing, *to take a photograph of the Queen's wreath and give copies to the parents of the deceased, free of charge.*

Wine glasses were engraved commemorating the disasters although with misleading information on the total number of children's deaths. Among the donors to the fund were the Canadian and Indian La Crosse team, who were touring England at the time. They had *'generously resolved'* to give the proceeds of their match, on July 6th to the bereaved. This splendid touring team contained players having the names of 'White Eagle' ' Hole in the Sky' 'Whispering Leaves' and ' Tree Fall Down.' Sounds like a formidable outfit, a team you wouldn't want to meet in a cup-tie on a wet and windy night. They had played before the Queen at Windsor and their matches had produced large crowds throughout their tour of England.

The entertainment business was not slow in blowing their own trumpet with donations.

The Cherry Ripe entertainment at St Johns Wood donated £1.5.6p

The distinguished Shakespearian actor Sir Henry Irving announced (quite loudly I would imagine) that he would be sending 20 guineas. Sir Henry Irving had made his stage debut at the Lyceum Theatre in 1860 and had not forgotten the kindness shown to him by the people of Sunderland.

At the other end of the society, a chimney sweep raised a guinea from an inn.

I have selected a few more donations to give a cross section of the people who helped to raise £5,770 by August 1883. A lot more was promised but not always collected.

Two Jewish boys from Bedford £2.14.8
The Anchor tube factory Birmingham £5
Lord and Lady Londonderry £70
Seven children from Newbury 7 shillings
Worthing Brass Band 8 guineas.
Mrs. Backhouse Ashburn Quakers £2.
The Singer Sewing Machine Company and employees _ £8.
The Scottish Floor Cloth Company £2 11 6.
The Marchioness Westmeath £2
The Dowager The Lady Lilford 8 guineas

Diamond hill board school 10s
Lambert & Co Great Dover Street London £110
The officials and workers Deptford Brass yard £3
A working man from Glasgow £3
The Oddfellows of Batley Bridge £2

Most of the large industries, ship makers, the glass factory, the collieries, the rope makers etc. situated in Sunderland and Newcastle added to the kitty, with some workmen insisting that donations should go to the families that had experienced loss and injury. This was due, no doubt, to the fact many of the deceased's fathers were employed in these factories. These industries continued to donate money weekly; such was the feeling of sadness that was felt by work comrades in the town.

Bibles presented by the London committee of the British Foreign Bible Society, considered to be *'handsome and valuable,'* were to be engraved and presented to the bereaved parents although the Maconkie family unfortunately had their surname spelt incorrectly. The famous Victorian Scottish poet William Topaz McGonagall, who seemed to revel in writing disaster poems, weighed in with a heavy poem which can be found at the back of this book in full. Other poems are also there for your consideration.

One of the problems that arose with the fund was that promises were counted as actual donations. It appeared that certain gentlemen of the town had promised to pay generous amounts but were a bit slow in coming forward. This meant that the running total was never a true reflection of what had actually been collected or what was still outstanding. The Relief committee soldiered on and came to a final agreement that the money accrued should be used for the following

1. Relief to the families involved in the calamity. (This to be dealt with immediately)
2. A monument to the dead children. (£250 only)
3. A convalescent home or children's hospital. (Depending on the amount donated)

Some grieving parents and relatives were showing concern that the personal preference of the committee was being promoted without too much thought of the dead children and recovering siblings.

To counter this the mayor was quoted as saying; *'I would simply say one thing. It was not an exaggeration to say that some 70/80 per cent of the money sent to him as Chief Magistrate had been spent expressly for the relief of those who had lost their children. Any monument to be erected was secondary consideration altogether.'*

It seemed that this statement was not agreeable to everybody. Members of the committee were certainly looking further afield. Mrs. Laing (whose husband belonged to the Laing shipbuilding family) promoted the idea of a convalescent home while Dr. Mordey Douglas a surgeon, obviously preferred the children's hospital option.

Meetings were coming thick and fast with a Mr John Cameron proposing that £100 should be allocated for the parents to help with the funerals and added somewhat ungraciously *'with that out of the way then the committee could decide what to do with the rest.'*

John Cameron was a keen botanist and took a prominent part in the establishment of the Sunderland Art Gallery. He died in Sunderland, November 10th 1901 and is buried in the town. (There was a plaster cast of him in the Sunderland Library.)

The Day the Children Fell Asleep

At the time, Cameron was well thought of by the workingmen of Sunderland but after these remarks he came down in their estimation drastically. When you considered there were at least 156 (numbers vary) families touched by the tragedy through death of their children, this amounted to just under £1 per household despite the fact that some families had lost 2, 3, even 4 children in the crush. In some cases the children were insured, this was quite common among the working classes due to the high mortality rate of young children. Members of the committee *'pondered if parents of these children should get any money at all'*. Also would parents be paid more for multiple deaths? There were other situations to be considered where families who had parents too distraught to attend work or having children so traumatised by the terrible events being unable to be left alone. Other expenses that parents experienced, although at times sneered at by committee members, still wanted attention. These were families living on very tight budgets and couldn't afford even the smallest outlay that would unbalance their finances. An example was given to the committee about Mrs. Robson a wife of a mason whose daughter Eleanor aged 7 had been killed in the crush. The mother was refused a refund on the cab fare of 1s 10p which she had paid to have her daughter brought home. (Some cabmen refused payment from the parents for these deeds of mercy but Mrs. Robson was not one of them.) The unfortunate woman also asked for help to assist in payment for a coat her son now needed. He had survived but his sleeves were torn from his coat (Mr. Bonner extricated him from the crush.) The boy was one of the last to be pulled out from outside the door. A Mr J. Homer (whose daughter was in the stalls and survived) was expected to be sympathetic to the parents. Later became the target of the parents anger when he visited some homes to *'dish out money'* for them, throwing it on the table 'like they were from the poor house.' It became chaotic at meetings for the bereaved families with dissent for the committee members was apparent. The families of the children killed caused disturbances at meetings by calling out *'They want the money for themselves.'* There was a feeling among the parents that the committee had endeavored not to *'deal handsomely'* with the fund at their disposal but to give as little as possible. It was generally thought the committee had already made up their minds to use the money for other purposes.

One parent announced at a meeting *' They had it made up before the bairns were coffined'*

History has shown us that the collection of money on behalf of working class victims soon became a source of envy and hate; it wouldn't be long before the bereaved became the accused. Even then the general public were turned against the victims, by the media, hearsay, lies and envy. Being readily informed that families are greedy, wanting to benefit from the deaths of their children and ridiculed for wanting a repair to a child's coat as the mother couldn't afford a new one. We had more unrest when the local papers had reported that the families were to receive £5 a head for the funerals.

Meetings arranged for the parents only progressed to the theme that they were not getting, what they thought was rightly theirs.

Mr Pringle (who had lost two daughters **Ann and Margaret)** said *'I do not care whether I get another halfpenny, but I feel offended and insulted by the remarks that had been made by Mr Homer which has caused me to leave my place of business on my busiest day to attend this meeting. I ask those who had* *grievances to get up and speak of them, so that the committee would have some arguments to use on their behalf.'*

A mother said she had got £2, but had expended £6 6d, and had paid the rest herself. Mrs Jane Ramsay, 36, Covent Garden-street, stated that Mr Homer had said that the next time he called he would bring money for her and all she got £3. Both her husband John and herself had been ill since. Mr Pringle encouraged the parents present by saying *'That's the way to speak out.'*

A parent remarked that he had heard that Mr Lane lost two children (Charles **Henry10 and James William 6**) and only got 10s. Mrs Lane said 'it was stated in the Echo that we had got £1, and she went to Mr Homer to query the amount and he showed her that the 10s was right. The undertaker's bill was £6 0s 6d.'

Another parent said his undertaker's bill was £6 12s, and he got £3, the relief committee stated that was right as *'He had gone to a lot of unnecessary expense.'*

Mrs Fairley, Covent-garden, said *'she had got £2.'* Mr Pescod, Burleigh-street, (who had lost two **children Margaret 10 and May Eleanor 5)** said his wife had been unwell since the calamity, that she had lost *'six stones of flesh.'*

William Downey, 5 Back Sussex Street lost a daughter **Mary Downey aged 7**,he had spoken to Mr Homer about the funeral expenses, and he got nothing but insults from that gentleman. Mr Davison (not sure if this is the father of **John Clark Davison** or **Martin H Davison**) said he had 'got nothing' and Mr Watson **(Lost Amy 13, Ann 10, Robert 12,)** had stated the same. A parent asked who Mr Homer was? He was only a man; let them as workingmen show the committee how to do it. (Applause.)

The Publican of Willow Pond Inn, Mr Wright (who lost **Mary aged 5**.) He said 'the undertakers' bills that had been sent to them, and every one was exceedingly exorbitant. It was something enormous the amount they had to pay for coffins. He had been in the trade himself and they could make good coffins much cheaper. The bill sent to him was 6 guineas. He argued that this should come out of the money given by the sympathetic public to the relief of the bereaved parents. He thought '*It was something scandalous if it wasn't.*'

Mrs. Bland, of 66 Hedley-street, who had lost William her 10-year-old son, said *'they did not get the Museum until the calamity at Seaham, and now they wanted a Convalescent Home through our disaster.*' (Laughter and stamping.)

There was a majority of opinion that the money was not being spent the way it was originally intended. This was tempered with warnings that if they made it a matter of cash, they would only be putting themselves in the hands of those who had written the shameful letters that appeared in the papers during last week. There was something like £5,400 gathered, but the editor of the Echo gently reminded them that not all of the money had been collected. If they put the sum down £2,000, and allowed for memorial stones, that left about £3,030, but deducting £1,000 for any other object, it left then £2,000, and they had every reason to believe that this was for the relief of the parents. Even given another £1,000 from this, allowed the parents the remaining £1,000. He urged upon them to stand together. Mr Davison thought that any child still suffering and also mothers who had received shocks from the effects of the calamity should be sent away and all expenses paid out of the funds. With reference to the amount per head for each child, he did not value his children that way. Mr Davison *added it was not for the committee to decide what was to be done with their money. It was the parent's decision.* A discussion then ensued, and it was ultimately agreed to write to the Relief Committee.

After some lengthy and careful consideration, the following suggestions were proposed for this meeting's consideration and action

(1) That we appeal to the Relief Committee, asking them for all reasonable expenses to be paid.' (Applause.)

(2) That considering the many expenses which we parents have been put to, in order to facilitate matters to an easy settlement, we appeal to the Relief Committee, asking them for the sum of £10 per head, believing this not to be an unreasonable sum. (Applause)

What also aggrieved the parents was that the Mayor at one of the earlier meetings was quoted as saying and often repeated

'I would simply say one thing. This was not exaggeration to say that some 70 / 80 percent, of the money sent to him as Chief Magistrate had been spent expressly for the relief of those who had lost their children. (This statement brought loud applause) 'Any monument to be erected was secondary consideration altogether.'

Later the fund raising committee released this statement to explain what the Mayor 'really meant.'

Actual and immediate necessities springing from the calamity had to be relieved, but the bulk of the fund was to be devoted some permanent commemoration of the general sorrow. This was the object of the fund from the first, and this, notwithstanding the Mayor saying that 80%, of the money he had received was given for the benefit of the parents, was the purpose reaffirmed by the General Committee last night. His

Worship-has now given explanation of his remark, which will generally regarded tantamount to a retraction.

In other words the families were not going to get anything like what they expected or promised by the Mayor.

The Lord gives and the lord takes away Job 1. 21

In the case of the widow Mrs Roper, whose daughter Mary was killed but also had another daughter in hospital. Mrs Roper was employed to wash and clean houses to raise money for the family. This had now become very difficult due to the fact that her son was affected by the trauma and couldn't be left alone for long periods, as he required constant reassuring, which at times prevented her from working. What compensation would she receive? What of her now only son who had witnessed his sister killed and another sister in hospital, would he ever forget their pleading for rescue? Life had certainly been cruel to Isabella Roper through no fault of her own; She surely could not be labelled as a 'scrounger.'

(In the 1911 census William was still with her, the two remaining daughters had married)

In my research I have found differing amounts given to the parents, which have varied from £10 per family and £2. 10 s for each child lost to £3.00 per family and 10s for each child loss. The agreed sum for the parents was given by most reports as being only £553. Many funeral expenses were considered in some cases as too extravagant and that some invoices had been *'tampered with.'*

Several letters were sent to The Echo describing the parents as *'money grabbers'* and *'having no shame'* There was also strong support for those who had witnessed the terrible event and still had that picture of distraught parents moving clothes away from small faces to be able to recognise their dead children. Many questions were asked and the letters continued to come in as confusion continued. This is a typical letter of the time that was unsupportive of the parents.

It must have been with feelings of indignation and contempt that the public read the report of the above meeting that is published in your issue of today. It is to be hoped that extraordinary conduct of the 'bereaved parents' can be accounted for by the "shock" from which one of the speakers said he was still suffering. No other ground it is possible to exonerate the chairman and speakers from blame. I feel sure that the committee will be acting contrarily to the wishes of the general public if it devotes any more money to the "relief of bereaved parents." In pecuniary sense, those persons must be more favourable situated than if their children were still living. Their household expenses will be less. If, as appears to be the case, some of those parents are so constituted that monetary assistance is alone able to soothe their anguish the loss of their children's companionship, I am exceedingly sorry for those of their children who were not killed in the Victoria Hall. I trust that no grumblings, protests, bullying on the part of those people will divert the committee from laudable object they have in view, that of erecting an institution which will be at once a record of the public sorrow. Yours truly, Samuel Kinsman. Warwick Street, Monkwearmouth.

I certainly hope that Mr. Kinsman was not assuming that working class parents had no feelings for their children and looked upon them as a household expense. Is he suggesting a family cull every now and then would be helpful for a working class family?

John Taylor

Mr Kinsman soon received a curt reply from William Browell

Sir, If were not for the fact that Samuel Kinsman's letter the above subject is calculated to mislead the public, I would allow it to pass with the silent contempt which it otherwise deserves, but as the inference which the public is likely to draw from the said letter is, that all the expenses of the funerals etc. Have been defrayed out of the Relief Fund, I cannot refrain from stating that such is not the case; on the contrary, the majority of cases an amount equal about three-fifths only of the undertakers bill has been given by the committee. If Samuel Horseman (local blacksmith) had furnished the funerals, and had received in return only the amount distributed by the committee, I inclined to think his "indignation and contempt" would have been considerably greater than, is at present, at the conduct of the bereaved parents. The most unkind and unsympathetic of his remarks " Some of them are so constituted that monetary assistance is able to soothe their anguish." What expression to emanate from anyone who was called a father. I wish to correct the idea on this matter, and to state that the object bereaved parents had, by calling the meeting, was to ascertain what was going to be done with the money that had been subscribed solely for their relief (which originally represents about 80 per cent, of the total amount subscribed), and not to endeavour to extort money as a solace, but simply to obtain what is their just due. Viz., a fair and discreet distribution of the money subscribed by the sympathetic public for the relief of the bereaved. I don't know what may be the opinion of others, but my own is that when money is subscribed for given purpose, ought to be devoted to that purpose, and that alone, —Yours faithfully, W. Browell. 3, Gilsland-street

(It is obvious that Mr Browell had not heard that the Relief Committee had now withdrawn the 80% offer.)

It was soon rapidly evident that the Relief Committee were not having working class parents telling them what to do or how to distribute money that had been donated. They hit back with venom and in a meeting stated that the mayor had received three anonymous letters criticising the action of the Relief Committee. He countered that no committee had worked more assiduously. He believed that such was human nature, *that if an angel was to come down from Heaven there were some men so critical that they would find some dusky feather in her plumage.* He did not believe in anonymous letters and if any more such letters were sent he would take no notice of them. He then went on to criticise the parents. *'There was something peculiarly repugnant to good taste, not to say decency, in the spectacle of bereaved parents clamoring for money in respect of lost children. The tone of the speeches was such as to repel rather than attract sympathy. It was querulous and undignified. It suggested too strongly 'perking in a glistering grief" and disposition to give a literal meaning to the phrase golden sorrow ran through all the plaintiffs spirit which was singularly unbecoming.*

The Relief Committee received such complaint as that not any compensation had been given to children who had clothes shredded in the throes of trying to escape together with charges, which can only be regarded as discreditable to those who made them. The committee was convinced there were outside agitators stirring up trouble but decided that it was only just that they should disassociate the bulk of the bereaved parents from the clique that has been *so pertinaciously* assessing the monetary value of their loss. *We feel sure that the mass of those who have been stricken so deeply would recoil from a proposal that they should play the huckster in respect of their bereavement.* They recognised the fact that the public, who had given their money to the fund, had no idea of attempting to compensate the parents who had 'sneered' by the disaster. The actual and immediate necessities springing from the calamity were to be relieved, but the bulk of the fund was to be devoted to some permanent commemoration of the general sorrow. This was distinctly stated. *The town is weary of the recent haggling for relief, and will be glad to see the matter settled*

So it seemed as though promises were made but never delivered. The town were told that they had got *fed up with these scrounging parents.*' The committee had come to sweeping statements about what the donors wanted doing with their money. Then concluded that they wanted, what the committee desired, without further conversations with workingmen or donors. The committee had given itself a headache by having so many sub committees. The parents were rightly demanding more money or the money that had been promised. The memorial statue was turning into a worse hangover than the sculptor was having. Many were not in agreement for a large monument as shown from this meeting at the Monkwearmouth Colliery, of the agents and the men. They passed a resolution *that the first object was the relief of all parents requiring it, and the second was the erection of a Convalescent Home.* The men did not favour the idea of a large monument. Several people were in favour of tablets placed at the three cemeteries that held the children

The convalescent home supporters wanted a large slice of the cake to get their project up and running. The idea of a children's hospital had been dropped without much discussion. The Victoria Hall calamity/ disaster committee it seemed was, rightly named.

Letters continued to come in with irate residents unable to contain their anger.

SHIPPING GAZETTE. Saturday, September 1884. A more miserable revelation of impotence and mismanagement than that brought to light at last night's meeting with respect to the proposed Convalescent Home can scarcely be conceived the most imaginative of men. It is fifteen months since the calamity took place. For the greater part of that time thousands of pounds have been lying, whilst other thousands are uncollected, and practically nothing has been done. An outcome solely resulting from want of business-like tact, energy, and directness of purpose.

Another queried the cold approach of the relief committee

The relief fund is fast becoming a public scandal. The responsibility for all this lies with the committee who have the large sum raised public sympathy for these in distribution. But the committee appointed to relieve them, without one spirit of that charity which '"believeth all things, all things, and endureth all things," intrude these poor people much in the same style as relieving officer does, poor whom adverse fortune has driven to seek parish relief. They are pestered even when time has not softened their heavy blow with all kinds of as their circumstances and expectations, instead of their expenses the matter cheerfully and liberally paid, the subscribers to the fund intended be, paltry dole £3 is awarded them. The committees must retrace their steps and award our poor townsmen every farthing they have been out pocket; it will remain for ever reproach to Sunderland connection with this dismal tragedy. W. Kerr.

Whilst a bereaved father explained how it affected him and his family

Dear Mr Editor, I will ask you, or any of your many readers, what (which I have got, and for which I thankful, out of the funds) would have done to have buried daughters, viz., undertakers' fees, mourning coaches, lie, mourning for four remaining children, aged mother, wife, and myself, loss of business (being a small shopkeeper), having had to close my shop shortly after the time of the slaughter of the innocents, on the colliery pay Saturday night, at six o'clock, and keep closed on the Monday and Tuesday following, and suffer the loss that many credit customers, I sorry to say, took advantage of deep grief and trouble, besides many other incidental expenses I would have been content with another sovereign, as told to Homer last week, but as I have been refused that amount, If my humble services will be accepted I will endeavour to get my share of what I am fully, justly, and rightfully entitled to, and see that my other poor sorrow-stricken brethren and sisters get the same; and then after that I with all heart will go in for a Children's Convalescent Home scheme, Sir, you will see that my position is not much improved taking circumstances into consideration, and I can only conclude saying shame, shame, shame upon such of the committee that hath striven to withhold the funds from the poor parents after having been generously, - freely, and given by the public for such purpose. Excuse trespass on your valuable space. J. A. Pringle. Southwick road.

Now all they had to decide was what were they going to do with the money after the monument and the families had been accounted for. It seems astounding that ten years later they were still discussing what to do with the rest. If we consider the Dunblane massacre where innocent school children were shot along with their teacher, their committee had to release a press statement that is printed below to bring an end to their misery.

After more than three years of intense scrutiny, the trustees of the fund set up to help people affected by the Dunblane massacre yesterday sought to end the attention focused on the community to allow it to rebuild fully. As the final audited accounts of the £5.2m fund, donated by well wishers and the government after the fatal shooting of 16 primary school children and their teacher, were published on the internet, it was revealed that details of payments are to be destroyed. No personal information recorded by the trustees will ever become public and even anonymous financial minutes will be held as closed records for 30 years. The trustees are determined to ensure that no one finds out who received money from the fund and to what extent they benefited from its resources. It is hoped that the winding up of what became a focal point for worldwide generosity in the weeks after the shootings of March 13 1996 will allow Dunblane to become just another town again.

Well that is one way to do it.

ಕಾಕಾಕಾ

Chapter 10
The Statue and Convalescent Home

John le Carrie once said that committees consist of members with four back legs.

Once the Relief Committee had told the families what they should expect to get, they passed on the poisoned chalice to the memorial team. A memorial statue was one of the first suggestions that the committee had agreed, although many workingmen preferred the option of tablets left at each cemetery receiving the dead children. It was left to the Memorial Committee to introduce some *'common sense'* into the project of producing a proper memorial to the children. A sculptor was found with tenuous Sunderland connections and a set price of £250 was agreed, a block of marble was bought, what could go wrong? What follows is an example of what can go wrong, when you are not paying attention.

A meeting of the Memorial committee as reported in local newspaper.

Dr. Cameron asked if the Mayor had any information as to the progress of the commemorative statue.

The Mayor: *I wish I could give any information. In October 1883 the order was given to a Mr. Brooker, and he was allowed two years for its completion. I certainly hoped I would have been able to speak with some certainty about it, but I am not able to say so tonight*

Unknown: *Has he got any money on account?*

Ald. Storey: *Will the Town Clerk or Mr. Thompson give us any information with respect to the matter, because they have seen Mr Brooke*r. (The Sculptor)

The Mayor: *I have seen him too.*

Ald. Storey: *Is it not fact that the committee has paid the whole of the amount it was authorised to pay (£200) and that the thing has not begun yet. That the artist had got the marble and says he has spoiled it, and that he does not intend to proceed further until you give him £60 or £70 to get another block of marble. I would like to know if that was the case?*

Thompson; *I only know that it was said in this room by someone, that they had seen the memorial, and that it was well advanced, and on this ground the money was forwarded.*

The Mayor: *Ald. Storey is right, and he is also wrong. I hope that the reporters will not take any notice of this matter, as it will do no good if this gets out to the public.*

Ald. Storey: *That is just what ought to be noticed, to show how the committee has managed the thing. The Mayor said nothing had been done, without, as they thought, due care. He knew little about Mr Brooker, but he was, by the unanimous vote of the committee appointed to execute this statue. He then received £125 on account, as he informed the committee that this was uniformly done when an artist received a commission to do work. Application was afterwards made by him for a further sum on account to enable him to purchase the block of marble that he required. By order of the General Committee it was awarded to* him. Some time passed, and he applied for a still further amount. Some time passed over and he applied for a still further sum of money. Before that was given to him, the sub-committee was empowered by, the General Committee to deal with Mr Brooker. Mr Thompson then went to the artist's studio in London, and saw an enlarged model, which was completed. Mr Brooker told him there had been a defect in the block of marble he had bought; it was either too small, or there was some flaw in the marble. They were afterwards told he would require another payment to enable him to go on with the statuary group. As he had already received £250, they did not pay him any more money. But by the vote of the committee £500 was the amount agreed to he given to Mr Brooker. They might say frankly they had been dissatisfied with him. He had not made that progress with the work that he ought to have done. He (the Mayor) had himself been to London, and seen Mr. Brooker, who assured him that no delay would take place. He might promise to the group that it would be done by next month. But that was now im*possible.

Mr Bowey (The town clerk) saw him next and his conversation with him was not satisfactory but he had the assurance of Mr Brooker's brother that the work would be duly executed in a manner that would give satisfaction to the committee. Mr Bowey added that if the sculptor had deceived them it had *not been their fault, but their misfortune.*

Mr Thompson referred to the minute book of the 11th November, where there was a record that the honorary treasurer was ordered to pay £125. Afterwards, Mr Thompson said, the treasurer submitted a copy of a financial statement, which contained a item that Brooker had been paid on account of the statue £175.

Ald. Storey: *Where is the order of the committee?*

The Secretary *The Finance Committee had the power to pay all the accounts.*

A Workman: *They certainly do not.*

Ald. Storey: *That is to say, you paid without any meeting of the committee. I wish that there should be no mistake about this, for I happen to know the facts. I voted against the expenditure of any money at all, but finally the committee decided to spend £250, and that is the only power that they possess. It is quite true that a later meeting had sanctioned 500 guineas expenditure, but only on condition that the subcommittee appointed should collect and be responsible for the extra money. That is on the minutes.*

The Mayor: *If Ald. Storey will only be fair and candid, I would not object to any remark he has to make, but I object to the one-sided way he has of putting things. He has only given part of the resolution. A number of gentlemen were appointed to act as a guarantee committee to raise subscriptions to the sum of 500 guineas " if any fault was found with the committee increasing the amount." Personally I am quite prepared to recoup the committee my share if required.*

Ald. Storey: *That's right. We will now get into the facts of the matter, because everybody who knows the facts is aware that Mr Brooker has used the money, and the work has not yet been done. The marble has never been touched. The Town Clerk, if he would, could tell us the facts, and I think something ought to be done to compel the fulfillment of the agreement (applause) for if we are not to have the convalescing home it would be too bad if in addition we did not get the memorial. I hope the Guarantee Committee will take the matter up, raise the rest of .the money, and compel Brooker to perform his contract.*

Bowey said as treasurer he had been placed in a somewhat awkward position, getting more awkward by the minute I would imagine. After the resolution to expend another resolution was passed that £500 guineas should be spent. He was aware of an understanding that if any of the subscribers should complain certain gentlemen in the town and members of the committee, would guarantee the amount. Under these circumstances, he argued, what was the treasurer to do? He said he had seen Mr Brooker personally and had his own doubts about the matter. *But what security could they get from a sculptor? (Laughter.)* An agreement was reached with him where we complied with the rules of the profession, which was to pay the artist a percentage (down payment) before he had done anything .He went on to say *Like the Mayor and the rest of them he was not altogether satisfied, and he hoped Brooker would advance little faster than he had done.' (Laughter.)*

The Mayor: *I have been told more than once that one or two gentlemen who have taken a very prominent part in this matter knew something of the antecedents of Brooker, and I complain of any gentleman who, having that knowledge, has not come here and put us on our guard against him.*

A workman representative asked the Mayor if it was not fact that when the Mayor went to London Mr. Brooker was drunk and had been for some time. (Laughter.) He gave it up as a lost job then.

The Mayor*: I don't think it is so. I have a letter from Mr. Brooker, who explains that he has a friend who is quite prepared to guarantee the money for the other block of marble provided we accept the work when it is duly completed.*

The meeting then terminated amidst the strongest expressions of condemnation by various workingmen representatives present at the businesslike conduct of affairs. Many of them declared that they would call meetings in the yards and workshops and demand their money back. They thought it only right that it should be used to relieve the present distress of the parents and surviving children. They argued that they preferred this, than supplying money for the artist to have another drink.

The public of Sunderland were not at all pleased, one man venting his fury in a letter to the Sunderland Echo.

September 1884.

It is fifteen months since the calamity took place. For the greater part of that time thousands of pounds have been lying, whilst other thousands are uncollected, and practically nothing has been done. Nay, worse than nothing. The first general meeting of subscribers it was resolved that after relieving the parents and helping the sick children, not more than £250 should be expended over a memorial. The remainder of the fund was to be employed in the establishment of a Convalescent Home. Is manifestly insufficient for this purpose. If vigorous efforts had been made in' a business-like way a year ago, the money might have been obtained, but the matter has, been allowed to drift and drivel on till in times like these it would be mere madness to appeal for the thousands needed. Such is the miserable outcome of this affair, an outcome solely resulting from want of business-like tact, energy, and directness of purpose.

It would seem that The Sculptor was indeed an alcoholic, and couldn't keep sober enough to even finishing an arm or a leg with a blunt chisel. The various members of the committee now had another problem on their hands when a letter was received in November 1885, nearly two years and half years after the children's deaths. There was no news that the sculpture had progressed any further but rather the opposite. It must have put years on the committee It read....

Esher, Surrey, Nov. 26, 1885. To his Worship the Mayor of Sunderland.

Will you kindly pardon the liberty I take in writing to you in reference to the 'Sunderland Disaster Memorial,' which remains in an unfinished condition owing to **the lamented death of the sculptor***, Mr Brooker, and as the Memorial Committee will doubtless wish to have the work finished with as little delay as possible, I venture to offer my services to carry out its completion, and beg to say that would do my best to complete the late Mr Brooker's model with all the delicacy and finish requisite in such a work. I do not wish to seem premature, or interfere in anyway with Mrs. Brooker's arrangements, but interview had with her yesterday, she stated that it was her wish, and it was also that of her late husband, that in the event of his death I' should be asked to finish his work. You may probably know that Mr Brooker was formerly my assistant, and as I have executed many public statues in Birmingham and other large towns, besides being sculptor to her Majesty the Queen, I trust my name is not unknown to you, and that you will be kind enough to mention my name to the Memorial Committee. My studio is at Esher is only about 2 miles from the late Mr Brooker's, and if the committee would honour me with a visit and inspect my works before they make their final arrangement, I should be very pleased. Under any circumstances, will you permit me to advise that the memorial be placed in competent hands, i.e., some one accustomed to execute works of a similar kind, the beauty of the completed work will in a great measure depend upon the finish bestowed it. —With many apologies for troubling you, I am, dear Mr Mayor, obediently, F. Williamson.*

The sculptor is dead long live the sculptor

A bit of a blow for the sculpture and sculptor but with this offer of help from such an accomplished artist, the furrowed brows of the committee must have been eased a bit.

The committee grabbed his offer with open arms and after visiting his studio in Surbiton and viewing his artistic prowess, they agreed a sum totaling £500. This included the payment to the previous artist for a marble slab but not for packaging or including transporting the completed statue to Sunderland.

Mr. Williamson finished the work nearly two years later in 1887. He reported that the finished statue came to £470 that left £30. It was suggested, (by whom we don't know,) that Mr Brooker's widow should receive the amount. This was duly accepted and passed by the committee. So in fact Mrs. Brooker got more from the fund for being married to a drunk, than the families who had lost 3 or 4 children in the calamity. It must also be noted that Mr Williamson was the uncle of the late Mr Brooker and had been his nephew's tutor. (In sculpting not drinking)

The committee then had the problem of bringing the statue from Surbiton Surrey to Sunderland, a journey of over 300 miles. How much that cost is unknown but the total expenses recorded was £217. (This could have also included members of the committee expenses for visiting the studio.)

When it arrived it was a typical reflective Victorian dramatic piece. There was no doubting the quality of the work or the expertise of the sculptor, but it was not to everybody's taste. Where it would be placed was another headache for the committee combined with the ongoing problem of money for the convalescent home.

In May 1887 it was transported from Surbiton, rather nervously, to its agreed place of rest in Mowbray Park. To protect this fine work of art, a glass canopy was erected over it

There it stood until 1929 when a scheme to move it to the Sunderland Museum building was rejected, but in 1934 it was moved to Bishopwearmouth Cemetery without its glass case. It remained there until it was moved yet again over sixty years later back to where it started, in Mowbray Park with its glass canopy restored.

But wait, what about the rest of the money collected what would become of that? The committee insisted that some money donated was specifically for the convalescent home and the plan for this should be pursued with undue delay. The idea of a children's hospital had been dropped completely. Once again the committee's urgency slowed, which was reflected, in the fact they were still discussing the project over 10 years later. (Sunderland Football club won three league titles during this period.)

If we accept the parents had been paid £553 and the sculptor, his wife and uncle over £500. That left in the kitty, according to the committee, a sum of over £4000. A figure of £6000 is nearer the amount, if considering uncollected promised donations.

The idea of a convalescent home had been kicked around in several meetings but had been kept in the thoughts of the committee since the tragedy occurred. This was largely due to the efforts of Mrs. Laing, who had suggested the project, at the first Memorial Committee meeting. She was the second wife of Sir James Laing and would bear him a remarkable 14 children, so she knew the worth of somewhere quiet to lie down without interruption. She was a leading light in the social life of

Sunderland and was especially active in promoting charitable events. Her husband was the President of the Sunderland Corporation a group who had also shown an interest in a home but lacked the capital investment. This sounded like a deal made in heaven, now that the decks had been cleared and that money for the parents and the sculptor had been accounted for, the convalescent home could now take center stage. It turned out to be a long running saga, lasting for nearly ten years before an opportunity for the weary committee to finally unload the donated money. This breakthrough was due to Sir James's son being connected to a gentleman in London. . After many years of hesitation and countless meetings Sir James Laing was proud to announce that a house in Harrogate had come on the market that would be suitable for the project. That the home was over 70 miles away did not seem to bother anyone

Originally the home was going to be a respite for parents and children who had suffered as a result of the calamity. This idea became overlooked as discussions continued with only a definite proposal that the home should include a wall memorial to the dead children. No mention on how parents, relatives and friends were going to find the time and afford to get there or how the traumatised children were going to react to being so far from the comfort of loved ones. Still, they had a wall plaque promised.

The house found, was owned by a John T Grey, who lived at 13 Belgrade Road London. He had the house built in 1870s for over £3,00 but was now willing to sell the property plus land for £2,200 at a loss to him of £1,000. The Sunderland Corporation was now in a position to buy the house with money donated by The Victoria Hall from the disaster fund. The expense of renovating the house into a more compatible building was £1,600 and also covered by the fund. Other expenses were included and the sum given was just over £4,000. The proposed home was described as being in Lancaster Park, High Harrogate, and fronting Wetherby Road. The committee was told *'The gardens are judiciously laid out and the surrounding trees greatly add to the situation.'*

In a committee meeting the final allocation of the Victoria Hall money was agreed and the resolution that the existing money in the fund should be given to the Sunderland Corporation for the project. The Mayor then formally moved that the accounts be received and adopted and carried. Councilor Addison was very much gratified that the proposal had been adopted unanimously. He believed it would bring unqualified satisfaction to the town that the money was to be appropriated in the way proposed. He moved that the hon. treasurer be, and hereby authorised, to place to the credit of the Infirmary Convalescent Home Fund the amount now standing to the credit of the Victoria Hall Disaster Fund. Councilor Coates asked if it was intended to hand over the whole of the money. The Mayor replied in the affirmative, and said they would see it was not desirable that Victoria Hall Disaster Committee should be continued. (Hear hear.)

Mr J. C. Moor was concerned about the question of maintaining in proper state the graves of the children the various cemeteries. It was put to the vote and the motion was carried but how much of the fund was given for this maintenance is not mentioned. So it was done, all the money gone and any future donations would go to the convalescent home. All that was necessary now was to organise a trip for everyone, who was somebody, to the opening ceremony. The Sunderland Echo set the scene

The Railway Company ran excursion with about 150 passengers, and during the morning about 70 ladies gentlemen, members of Victoria Hall Disaster Fund Committee, the Infirmary Committee, Workmen's Governors, and others left on the Leeds express, the Mayor having kindly provided three handsome saloons for their accommodation. On arrival and welcoming, an adjournment then took place to a large marquee which had been pitched upon the ground attached to the Home, and hereby the hospitality of the Mayor and Mayoress. The guests wore entertained at a sumptuous lunch purveyed by Brothers, of Sunderland. The weather all day was beautifully fine, in fact, a hotter day for the proceedings could not be imagined.

After lunch and speeches, at about 2.30, guests and trippers were gathered together and the Mayoress was called forward to accept the golden key to open the home. To *loud applause* we are told.

Having received the key, she fully performed the ceremony, and then, speaking from the steps, she added *the home would supply a long felt want, and felt sure they would all unite with her when she said that pleasanter and happier use could not have been made for the Victoria Hall Disaster Fund.*

Then on the train and back to Sunderland, in time for tea.

On September 15th 1894 a foundation stone was being laid at the new wing of the Heatherdene Convalescent Home, so naturally a train journey was on the cards.

A train left for Harrogate with a party of eighty, where they arrived at 12.30 p.m. They then proceeded to the Harlow Manor Hydropathical Establishment, where they ate a hearty lunch. Mrs. Laing was the guest of honour and had been invited to lay the foundation stone. It was a popular choice as Mrs. Laing for many years (eleven to be precise) had been a driving force to have a convalescent home dedicated to the children. This sentiment had become clouded over the years as most of the children affected by the disaster were now in their teens. (It is very doubtful if any of the children attended the home.) It was accepted that the home would now take in adults from a larger area, not just Sunderland and not just children. Mrs. Laing was presented with a beautiful silver trowel, upon which was engraved, Presented to Mrs. Laing by the Committee of the Sunderland Infirmary on the occasion of her laying the foundation stone of the new wing at the Heatherdene Convalescent Home, September 15tb 1894. Mrs. Laing then performed the ceremony of laying the stone, which she declared to be '*well and truly laid.*'

The men from Sunderland with their love of a committee decided that an annual visit to Heatherdene Home was appropriate just to keep an eye on their investment. No doubt proceeded with a luncheon. How many of these visits took place I do not know I have knowledge of three but there could have been more. Two men of the Relief Committee were voted onto the Sunderland Corporation Infirmary Committee and that in relation to the fund, was the end of it.

The history of the home includes the period during W.W.1 when Marie Georgievna Romanov better known as The Imperial Duchess of Russia was in England. On the announcement of the commencement of the war, The Imperial Duchess was on holiday in England and staying at Buckingham Palace along with the Tsar's mother. Her two daughters were in Harrogate receiving treatment for a mysterious illness. Although prompted by the King that she should return to Russia, she moved to Harrogate to be close to her daughters. She was so upset by witnessing the returning wounded and mentally ill soldiers, from the front, that she forced the British government (probably greatly influenced by the King) to open Heatherdene Convalescent home along with four other smaller homes for the benefit of the soldiers. She helped with the nursing and no doubt came into contact with men from Sunderland, as an agreement was in force that during the war, patients had to include men from there. Over 1200 men were treated during the conflict. Clanny Street where fatalities and injured in the Victoria Hall calamity were high, were reflected in the deaths and casualties during this shocking war. Many of the injured men of this street attended Heatherdene for respite. How gratifying that a fund with donations from Sunderland people should have benefitted and given care and medical attention to the soldiers, who were relations of the dead children. The home was taken over by the National Health, in 1948, with still a *'gentleman's agreement'* in place, to admit patients from Sunderland and local convalescents on a fifty/fifty basis. The home was demolished in the 1960s and is now a car park. All that remains is the original gardener's cottage.

There is a memorial on the road to Wetherby. It stands about a mile from the Great Yorkshire Showground in Harrogate. It stands about 7ft. tall and looks over the parkland. Inscribed are the names of the nine men who died of wounds in the hospital of the Grand Duchess George of Russia during the Great War 14 - 18

Jonathan Owen, Percy Meadwell, Ramsden Farrar, William Bailey, John E Robinson, Oliver Sewell, William Thomas, William Fenton, Arthur J Crook. and those who after leaving the hospital fell on the field of battle.

The inscription continues with, I am the resurrection and the life. He that believeth in me though he were dead yet shall he live. John11: 25

The Heatherdene Home Harrogate with the extension

Chapter 11
Who was looking after them?

Hillsborough 1989

When the gates were opened, thousands of fans entered a narrow tunnel leading from the rear of the terrace into two overcrowded central pens, creating pressure at the front. Hundreds of people were pressed against one another and the fencing by the weight of the crowd behind them. People entering were unaware of the problems at the fence; police or stewards usually stood at the entrance to the tunnel and, when the central pens reached capacity, directed fans to the side pens, but on this occasion, for reasons not fully explained, they did not. News reports conjectured that if the police had positioned two police horses correctly, they would have directed many fans into side pens, but on this occasion, it was not done.

The London Chronicle 1883 Victoria Hall

Ask why there was not a single constable on duty (at the hall) and say it is plain that the regulations respecting public buildings in Sunderland were surprisingly defective.

The Daily News 188

Is it misleading the Sunderland public to describe the Sunderland disaster as an accident, unless the word, clearly understand to include misfortune which we have not taken the trouble or had the foresight to provide against.

The crush at Hillsborough in 1989 was where 96 Liverpool supporters lost their lives. Events at the Victoria Hall were similar to this, with the same calamitous outcome. Many football fans can remember attending matches in older stadiums, where once inside the stadium, they were left to get on with it. The occasional steward might help in locating your seats but for standing areas you did the best you could. In the seventies I was attending a game at White Hart Lane in the Park lane enclosure considered to be a 'Tottenham end.' Tottenham were playing Chelsea and during the game a group of Chelsea fans revealed themselves and began chanting. This aggravated the Spurs fans and they turned to face them. A crush occurred as some fans tried to get away from the trouble. Police intervened and many people were evicted. At the end of the game we made our way to the exit. Suddenly the crowd rushed towards some Chelsea fans that had been missed by the police. Several of my friends and I were taken off our feet and were then at the mercy of where the crowd had intentions of heading. This lasted several seconds until we reached double doors that allowed us to spill out into Park Lane. To be part of a rush without any control on what was happening was truly frightening. We laughed about it afterwards but for a few seconds I experienced how those caught up in a crowd rush realise that once a herd moves in one direction and panic sets in, it is virtually impossible to stop them.

Sunderland had never before hosted a show, which had attracted so many children eager to attend. Originally there was a generally accepted public opinion that the schools had distributed the 'tickets' for the show, but this was not true. A Mr Hetherington in a letter to the Sunderland Echo said that he had visited two of the main schools in Sunderland. Both headmasters denied giving out these tickets/advertisements to the children. At the inquest a headmaster George Carr Watson of St Paul's School admitted that he had distributed some to his pupils and teachers. He pointed out they were 'advertisements' for the show and the children still had to get money from their parents to attend. So if the parents didn't want them to attend, the children wouldn't go. He felt no responsibility, as Saturday was a holiday, he added rather sarcastically *'A holiday all day.'* He pointed the finger at the parents, saying it was up to them whether the children attended. He confirmed *'this wasn't a school-instigated excursion.'*

The Victoria Hall calamity began by the isolation of the 22-year-old Charles Hesseltine and expecting him to contain children, running along that corridor, once the promise of a prize had been relayed to them. If proper stewarding and risk assessments, which is paramount today, had been carried out before the commencement of the show the danger would have been greatly reduced. Had the fatal door been left open and 'bolted back' the crushing would have been avoided. (We must remember it is very easy to judge an event in 1883 by the rules and science we have in place and understand today. It is still a case of 'ifs and ands.' When we consider that the total of children in the gallery was roughly 1,200 then today a minimum of twelve stewards would have been stationed to keep order and to assist in the vacating of this part of the theatre. It was reported by Mr Fay that adults and teachers were present although not one of these came forward to give evidence at the inquest or gave descriptions of the crush to the newspapers. Mr Fay later contradicted his observation by stating he had to go to the gallery at the interval to attend to some unruly children. Where were the teachers and parents? The next point was the inadequacy of control after seating these children into the gallery. It appeared from all the witnesses that there were few adults in the gallery. Witnesses put the number of adults ranging from two to eight. Fay gave the reason for filling the gallery was because he wanted the dress circle for the 150 school teachers, and finding he could not hire it (too expensive) he positioned them in the stalls. Children who had paid a penny readily occupied the gallery. (There is no evidence that 150 schoolteachers attended either in the stalls or gallery.) The organisers freely admit that no application was made to the Chief Constable for any assistance to keep order. Fay had undertaken to keep the safety, of those children in the theatre, with the force he had, a total of five men. Even this statement is debatable since Mr McClelland was not ordered to attend and according to his evidence had just turned up. Although Fay maintains that he was promised 'a checker' by the office, all a bit confusing.

The rush, which ensued, was left to one man to control. He panicked and why not, he was young and inexperienced in handling large groups of children and in his fright he allowed the door to close and the bolt to drop although he swears he didn't know of the bolt. This led to the fatal eighteen-inch gap, which only allowed just one child at a time, to exit the gallery. The unfortunate Hesseltine, who on a couple of occasions collapsed, was another one of the team, who had received no proper instructions and was therefore not up to the job. It would appear that the door was installed to help with crowd control and the taking of money, rather than crowd safety. The safety rule now applied to the density of people is 5 persons per square metres. This would allow 25 children to be safe in the 7ft x 7ft landing by the fatal door. It was estimated by the rescuers that there was about '300' contained on the landing and the stairs to a height of about six feet. This illustrates how tightly crushed the children had become.

To have so many die in such a small space needs explaining. Their deaths would have been brought about by actual expulsion of air from the mouth by pressure upon the ribs and prevention of the movement of the chest necessary for breathing. (Trampling that is often reported in the media rarely causes a large numbers of deaths.) Crowd forces can reach levels that are almost impossible to resist. Evidence of bent steel railings after several fatal crowd incidents show that forces more than (1000lb) can occur. Forces are due to pushing, and the domino effect of people leaning against each other. If you have three minutes where you are unable to oxygenate your brain, you suffer significant brain injury. Another two or three minutes and you die. When you can't lie down, because when you faint you are supposed to collapse, you die a cardiac death because there is no blood supply to the head. This can be easily explained by realising that trampling occurs when pedestrians are in motion. Crushing occurs when a moving crowd (the children exiting the gallery) come into contact with a stationary crowd (The children stuck behind the door) Professor Keith Still who was involved with the Hillsborough inquiry bluntly stated ' When flesh and bone meets steel and stone there can only be one outcome'

Once the crowd of children started panicking, worrying they would not get a prize, they begun pushing and shoving you then have an incredible escalation of fear. When the density of a crowd increases, the normal order of a crowd decreases.

The added problem of the age of this audience means, from a rescue perspective, it is as bad as it gets. This is borne out by the difficulty the rescuers had extracting children from the massed throng.

'*We were frightened we might break their bone*' and pleas from the trapped to '*get me out first*' had to be ignored.

The rush brings more of them together doing the same thing, (trying to find an escape) and the risks of quite serious consequences. So as soon as the rush began and the panic started the young children stood no chance. Only luck would allow less than 40% of the throng to survive. Only the quick thinking of the hall keeper to open the dress circle door and to direct children to safety, saved the lives of hundreds. In that small space behind the closed door, where older children obeyed their mother's orders by holding on to their younger sibling's hands, only good fortune would allow one to live and the other to die.

Today it is generally agreed, that one in 100 ratio of crowd controllers to patrons is usually sufficient to keep a large crowd in check. But there are other mitigating factors, including the need for enough entry and exit points to manage the flow of the crowd. Although we often complain of 'health and safety gone mad' in the case of The Victoria Hall it would have saved lives. It was assumed by the organisers that the promise of prizes would be enough '*to keep children in order.*' In fact the exact opposite was the case. The hall keeper Graham, had some idea that the children were going to be a problem by asking Mr Faye's manager during the show '*who is in control of the children when they leave?*' At the conclusion of the show he started to clear children from the stalls and out of the theatre via the Toward road entrance. Due to experience in vacating the gallery he realised that not a great number of children had exited from the stairs above. He had misgivings and went to investigate, unfortunately by then it was to late for some.

The long awaited inquests were announced where it was hoped that the truth would come out. Previous evidence given by the people attending could be scrutinised and any new evidence examined. The Bishopwearmouth began their inquest on July 2 1883. The Monkwearmouth began theirs on 9th July 1883.due to the dissatisfaction of the inquiry on the 'south side of the river' It was hoped by the Sunderland community that both inquests would shed light and even solve who (if anyone) was responsible for the tragedy but most of all would bring a conclusion to this tragic event. They were to be disappointed.

This summary below is a combination of both inquests and any new evidence that hadn't been produced before or differed from previous statements given.

We had the evidence of Mr Hugh Shield, QC. M.P. who attended the inquest on behalf of the Home Secretary into the deaths. Mr Shield offered the following in regard to the question posed' how came the swing door to be closed and bolted?'

I am unable to state with confidence to any conclusion other than that which was expected in the verdict of the jury, viz., that the evidence was not sufficient to determine it. Without intending to judge severely the evidence of the children, I think it would he unsafe to rely on the accuracy of their statements as to seeing Hesseltine put down the bolt. On the other band there are some proved facts and some probable inferences that appear to favour Heseltine's story. If the swing door was moved so far as the socket, it was in the highest degree probable that the bolt would fail into the socket.

This is a point that could be argued, Graham had closed the door 24 times and the bolt fell in once, Mr Fay claimed that he had tried 12 times and it had fallen in eleven times. (Well he would say that wouldn't he) Hugh also explored the theory that Hesseltine had in fact pulled the door behind him to regulate the flow of children and the bolt fell in to the socket without him knowing. Shield went on to say

I concur in the re- commendation of the jury that the swing door should be removed. It was not in the hall as originally built, but was added in 1876, without consultation of the architect, Mr Geo. C. Hoskins, who stated in evidence that he would not have sanctioned it. They appear to have thought of nothing in relation to the audience but the collection of the money.

Frank Caws a local Architect gave a very detailed observation of the hall, although admitting he didn't know there was a door where the accident occurred. He added that prior to the accident he would not have seen any danger to the audience, providing that the hall was properly managed. He went on to explain

That there was in actual fact two exits e from the gallery from an East and a West side, leading to two staircases, one on the east side and the other on the west side. That on the east side is the one generally used, and the one on which the accident happened. I would call the west entrance or stairs a relief staircase. It does not connect to the east staircase. It might be termed the panic egress, and is a very ample staircase. It admits the audience of the gallery to the lobby of the dress circle. They would then descend by a few direct stops into Toward Road. This west stair appears never to have been used and the east stairs seem to have been sufficient. Besides the main entrances there was a third into the pit on the northeast side from the platform entrance. As regards the arrangement of the doors, **they open outwards.** *In my opinion the hall is uncommonly well provided with exits under ordinary circumstances it would take about 5 minutes for the staircase to empty the gallery? The distance from the top of the gallery to the stairs out into the street is about 85ft. The total length is 42 people by 4 people in width, and by moving at once that makes 168, showing that if you pass people out in that comparatively comfortable fashion there would only be 168 or 200 passing out at once at two miles an hour. If the west staircase had been opened there can be no doubt that there are sufficient exits*

Of course this statement does not consider the excitement and age of the audience. The reported experiment of closing the door to see if the bolt fell in is not really acceptable. The bolt was according to several witnesses as twisted like '*a corkscrew*' after the accident and was only forced out by *two able police officers*. Unless they fitted an exact bolt to the door, a reconstruction would not have proved anything. Mr Fay admitted in earlier statements he was not aware there was a door so he couldn't have experimented with the bolt, before the accident and would have little time after the calamity. His manager, Wybert also said he didn't know that there was a door on that landing. Not forgetting that Hesseltine denied all knowledge of the bolt and only knew of the door when it started to close. We can assume from this that the door was open as the children arrived and when they begun to exit. We are left with, according to the evidence given, that only Graham knew about the bolt due to his constant use of the gallery and its likelihood of falling into the hole. Graham's statement of, one in 24 times was probably accurate, someone placing the bolt into the hole is more likely than the bolt falling into the hole accidently. (Graham had also said that the bolt was 'rather stiff' to push into the hole) In this evidence we see the first mention of another staircase, the west one, which could have been used. It would appear the west staircase was never used due, no doubt, to the lack of staff.

Now is a good time to review Fay's evidence, originally he was quoted as saying he did not know of the crush and returned home to Tynemouth that night. He then returned the following morning to pick up his equipment. Then he said to a newspaper that he had reached the train station where he heard of the accident and returned. Obviously this would not fit with other evidence to be given so he eventually said at the inquests that on hearing (from Hesseltine) that children had died and been injured, he rushed outside to find medical men to help the children.

He was asked 'Did you find one?'
'Yes just outside the hall'
'How did you know he was a Doctor?'
To which Fay replied ' he looked like one.'

(That would be the only bit of good fortune he had experienced that day). Previously in a statement by his assistant Hesseltine, which led us to believe that Fay was with him helping to extract children from behind the door. We can dismiss this as no other witness puts him there and later Hesseltine did not repeat this story at the inquest. (Fay and Hesseltine gave the same address as 35 Percy Street Tynemouth at the inquest.) Fay was also asked to the position of the bolts on the doors, he said that they were all lengthways and the doors opened outwards. (Of those he admitted he know about) He added that it was not his responsibility for the safety of the children; this was the duty of the proprietors. When asked if he returned to Tynemouth that night he replied, no he returned to the hall at 10. 30 but did not reveal where he had been in the meantime.

The only witness to the event whose evidence hadn't been widely reported earlier in a newspaper was that of Jane Graham the hall keeper's wife. She stated that she had washed the stairs of the gallery on Friday night and the door was open against the wall, opposite the fateful stairs. She said that if it had been shut off she would not been able to open it from that side. She would have had to go via the dress circle to release a bolt from the wall. ('*I would have remembered doing that.*') Jane was also adamant that she had told Mr Fay's sister that a few latecomers, all children, were allowed to enter. Under oath she said she couldn't recall hearing Mr Fay's request *not to admit any more to the gallery*. It would seem strange that the organiser of such an event would not want more paying customers, as this would only bring him extra revenue. At no point was he concerned about the safety of the children until at the end of the show, when he is reported to have said '*Distribute the toys at the gallery doors to avoid a crush*.' We must not forget that he had just one man there to carry out this order, as Wybert didn't arrive until much later.

Another witness to give evidence was the Victoria Hall owner Mr Frederick Taylor, who for some reason had been awarded a seat at the coroner's table; he commenced his evidence with a joke.

The Coroner: What profession are you?

Taylor: I am of no profession. I hope I am a gentleman. (Laughter.)

This set the scene for his evidence; a sense of indifference surrounded him. When asked to swear that a statement was true he brought more light relief by saying 'I don't swear.' He said that he was in his office at 11.30 but was not aware that the hall had been booked for that afternoon. He left the town shortly afterwards so was not aware of the accident until later. He also added that he was unaware of any agreement made with Mr Fay of a 25% extra payment of the takings to be paid to him. (He must have been thankful that his name was positioned on the coroner's desk as he might have been unaware where he was sitting.) His sworn (affirmed) evidence included *I am simply the owner, and if you wish to know of any arrangement with Graham, the arrangement is that he shall look after my interest, but he is not responsible for those who take the hall. When they take it they are my tenants for the time being, and are responsible for the use of it.*

When questioned about the suitability of the door he said

It has proved that it has done no mischief until, through a combination of peculiar circumstances this result has arisen

Mr Shield: Don't you think this door liable to be unobserved?

Taylor; *as they go up the stairs they must see it. It is so conspicuous an object that I can hardly understand how any man could pass through and not see it. I heard one professional man say so, and I was astonished. I certainly think after what has occurred some alteration is desirable, not because it is in itself dangerous, but because it has proved a source of mischief. I am of the same opinion that the door was not unwisely put up.*

A Juryman asked what are your instructions to the caretaker?

Taylor; His duty is to attend to my interest, to be as serviceable as possible so far as the comfort of the audience is concerned, but to hold aloof from all responsibility.

According to Mr Taylor he had no knowledge of the business that went on at the Victoria Hall and left most of the bookings etc. to his agent Mr Howarth: lets see what he had to say.

Howarth began by admitting he was not at the hall and he didn't know of the engagement or the people's names involved. He also didn't know about the accident until about an hour after the show had finished. (Six o'clock)

The Coroner asked him: Did *you know that Mr Coates had any share in Fay's entertainment?*

'I have asked him repeatedly if he had, and he has emphatically denied that he had anything to do with it. Had he had anything to do with it, I would have thought it extraordinary that he had not mentioned the matter to me.'

So we have another person who swears under oath that he knew nothing about the entertainment going on at the hall. Despite the fact that the hall was booked on the Thursday and that Graham was told of the confirmation of the booking at Coates's office on Saturday at about 10 or 11 (Graham was at the office twice that morning.) Howarth agreed, with Mr Taylor, that he never knew of any extra payment to be paid, other than £2. 2s. (For the renting of the hall.) He assumed only **this** amount would have been collected by Graham.

So we have two people, who were in the office on that Saturday morning, yet knew no knowledge of a show going on at their hall despite the business being carried out whilst they were there. Next the inquest heard from a reluctant 16 year old, Mr McClelland an office clerk to Hayworth. He lived with his widowed mother in Derby Street where his mother ran a girl's school. This was about a 10-minute walk from the hall.

According to him he just wandered into the hall, as it was close by, to have a look round. What has he got to say about himself?

Hugh Shield: You had some conversation with Mr Fay?

Yes, at the commencement.

Did you represent yourself to Mr Fay as willing to help in keeping order amongst the children? No

He said nothing about it? No

Mr Fay considered that he had a staff of four people who were prepared to assist, and whose duty it was to keep order— Hesseltine, you, Wybert, and Graham. Were you ever given to understand by Fay that you were one of his staff upon which he relied to keep order?

McClelland: He never said anything of the kind.

The Coroner: What payment were you to receive? You went to the hall to get an engagement, and you do not engage to give up your Saturday afternoons to work for nothing. You expected Fay would pay you? Yes

A Juryman: Whom did you represent? No one.

A Juryman: Did you not represent Mr Coates? No.

A Juryman: Did you do it as a favour for Mr Coates? No.

Mr Newlands: Did you know that Coates, having to go out of town, could not go himself, and therefore sent you?

No: I heard that from him afterwards

His other evidence included that he endorsed the fact that Graham was told on Thursday he 'could be needed' to open the hall on Saturday afternoon but they would confirm later. (Which they did on Sat.) Mr McClelland in a moment of youthful innocence added that he heard Mr Coates tell Graham to take a fourth of the proceeds of the entertainment for the hall. He understood it to be for the proprietor of the hall, not for Mr Coates. After giving such revealing evidence I am not so sure that McClelland was employed for very much longer. He was just 16 years old when he gave this evidence so could have been considered unreliable. If we are to believe him that it was not certain he would turn up on Saturday that would have left Fay with only three men at his disposal.

Mr Coates was introduced to the fray and if the jurors were not confused they soon would be. After much toing and froing from the Coroner and Mr Coates on whether he and Mr Hayworth were agents of Mr Taylor the Coroner started

When did you first see Mr Fay about the letting of the hall?

He met me in the hall on the 5th or 7th of June, and accompanied me to the office.

You saw Mr Fay on the Thursday, the 7th I think?

I think it would be the 7th, and he asked me for the earliest vacant days. I gave them to him

Did you on this day fix on a Saturday afternoon performance?

No.

When did the engagement take place?

I cannot say exactly. There are so many people calling to engage the hall.

I am glad to hear it. They will not call so frequently now. When did he take the hall?

On the Saturday, about one as far as I can recollect.

How odd 'about one' when Graham and McClelland put it at 10 or definitely 11 in the morning and only as a confirmation. It would take some believing that Fay and his entourage would set out from Tynemouth with all the equipment to a hall in Sunderland, rolling up at 12.30 when according to Coates it hadn't yet been booked.

He was questioned on the safety of the hall and the amount of adults present at the hall not forgetting he wasn't sure if McClelland was turning up.

Coates: After the hall is taken, I consider that I have nothing to do with it. I take no more interest in the transaction until I receive the money in payment; I considered that it did not rest on me, but upon the entertainer.

Coroner: Someone must be responsible for seeing to the safety of such a large number of children? Are you then satisfied that Mr Fay was responsible?

Yes. I asked him what staff he had, and he said that he **had an ample one.**

Who do we believe? As in Fay's sworn testament it had included

Coroner: *Did they ask you how many men you employed to assist you in the performance?*

Fay answered **'They never asked me.'**

Coates was then questioned about the fatal door.

You did not expect to find any door where the fatal door is?

No, certainly not.

Was the statement of the hall-keeper true when he said yesterday that before the performance commenced you, on Mr Fay's instructions, went downstairs and absolutely opened that fatal door?

There is not the slightest truth in it.

The Coroner: Did you open the street door? Yes.

Did you go down the gallery steps to open the street door? No. I went down the other way.

What other way? He wasn't asked. Surely he had to go down the stairs to the Laura street exit to open it? (The door only opened outwards) It seemed everyone was trying to distance themselves from the door by denying any knowledge that one existed. This denial also relieved them of having any knowledge of the infamous bolt. There is one basic question that should be asked, who was the last person to pass through the door. It was Hesseltine, as he admits in his sworn evidence *I went up the gallery stairs via the Laura Street entrance with the toys,* In that case the fatal door must have been open. When the gallery is not in use it is locked and can only be opened from the gallery side via the dress circle. (As testified by Jane Graham) He makes no comment that he had to do that. We know of children swinging on it before the performance but have no knowledge of anyone bolting it back against the wall. This was a heavy door it would have held its position until a mass of children got behind it and pushed it or it was dragged and finished up locked to the floor. Lets examine the 22-year-old Charles Hesseltine sworn evidence to see if that can assist in coming to a conclusion. I will print all the conversation regarding the encounter with the door and children. This is the most important description of the accident by the man who witnessed it all. He is under oath don't forget

Coroner*: Where did you meet the children coming down the gallery stairs?*

At the landing above the dress circle, going from the dress circle lobby.

That is a considerable distance above the fatal door?

Two or three landings

Did you give them anything there?

Yes; and I turned round with them, and as they came down I came down with them. Handing out prizes, I could not stand still.

You came down with the children?

Yes.

Were the children increasing in numbers as you came down?

Yes: they seemed to come down very quickly.

Jury man; there was a thicker and thicker crowd of children accompanying you down?

Yes.

Coroner: They went on increasing all the way down?

Yes. When I got to the dress circle that is on the passage landing they seemed to stop in front of me.

You stopped for some space of time on the dress circle landing?

Yes.

Then what did you do?

I shouted out, pass along, then some of them, I can't say who, shouted from round the corner, we can't! I thought perhaps some children had got a fright, or perhaps some had fallen on the steps and the others were waiting till they got up. When I got to the door it was half way open, and I am certain it was loose then.

Were you distributing prizes all the way down and when you got to the landing where the door is, you make a final stand?

Yes, I stood there. As I got to this door it was standing halfway open, so I went right down, and some of them seemed to make a way for me and some did not, and the moment I got halfway they seemed to wish to follow me, and just for a moment they put me in the door and held me there. I squeezed through and said, " Stand back, and don't get behind the door.

Hesseltine admits as he was nearing the door it was half open but didn't want to pass through. He wanted to stand and give out presents at that landing but the children had now got in front of him. The increase in children and pressure forced him squeeze through the ever-diminishing gap. The gap reduced presumably because of the weight of the children closing the door.

Hesseltine: After I got outside and told them to look quick and pass through, several of them said, I am waiting for my brother and sister. The press seemed to stop just for a moment then I thought I could get them all out. There seemed to be a break of children on the stairs. There seemed to be no more coming for a moment.

Coroner: *How do you think the door got from the position in which it was, when you went upstairs with the prizes, to the position of being ajar?*

I have not the least idea. I cannot account for it in any way.

The Coroner: *Did you attempt to get the bolt out?*

I did not know there was a bolt there. If I had known at the time, when there was not such a rush, I could have got it out easily.

Mr Newlands: *You say that at the time of the crush of the door, .you were not aware of it's formation .Not whether it was a swing door and could be opened on either side?*

Hesseltine: I did not know what to make of the thing. I first thought about getting the children out. I did not know at anytime time it was a swing door. I was outside the door and they were behind it. I gave one little girl a prize because she put her leg right round and someone squeezed her out. One got under another, and they put their arms through and I pulled them out.

Coroner: How do you explain these children telling us you were outside the door and that you put the bolt in?

Hesseltine: It is false, sir. I will swear it is false. I admit I was outside the door a long time, and I remember putting my hand down a lot of times to take the children away and pull them through.

Another witness admitting, that to begin with, he had no knowledge of the door or the bolt. When you read his statement it is nearly 3 weeks after the event and he has had time to think about it in a calm environment. This may have also allowed him to fit in favourably with other people's evidence. Graham testified, that at the time, Hesseltine was in a state of collapse that he looked spent and was petrified. He was standing at the opening of the door, slightly inside it, and was pulling at the children who were jammed against the door. Graham said because Hesseltine was' *much overcome*' he pulled him away and took his place. We know Hesseltine then rushed frantically down the stairs to find Fay who was still on the stage clearing away his equipment. This is where the distraught man collapsed and for a time couldn't speak. It wasn't until Fay had thrown some water in his face that he recovered. What is telling, is the evidence that children eager for presents surrounded Hesseltine and he had to rush towards the door, which we are led to believe, he thought would close shut like an ordinary door. By keeping it open he thought he could cope and for a time he could, until a fresh avalanche hit him. What occurred in those 10-15 minutes I don't suppose he remembers clearly? To his credit he did pull some children to safety but he was a young man at the time under so much pressure. At the inquest he was attempting to relieve himself of blame. He would not work again for Fay and I doubt if he ever got over this dreadful experience. He was put in a position that no one would have come out with glory. Although he was the last person who could have prevented the accident, he like the children, had no one watching his back.

Mr Wybert, Fay's manager was up next.

Wybert: *I arranged for the use of the hall on the 16th on sharing terms.*

Coroner: What do you mean by sharing terms? Who did you arrange with?

Wybert; Mr Stephen Coates, in Mr Howarth's office. He was to take a fourth of the gross receipts.

The Coroner: You stated that you expected a fourth of the proceeds going to the proprietors would carry with it an obligation, on the part of the proprietors, to see to the safety of the audience. Is that a specific bargain?

It is a general custom. If they take a fourth, they generally find the attendants and the money-takers, as the case may be.

It would appear that the management of the hall, by denying they had a deal with Fay could then hand the responsibility for attendants and safety to him and his manager. There is no doubt that if the entertainment had gone smoothly this money would have been paid and gratefully received. The 25% sharing agreement was not cleared up even when Fay's manager sent a postal order to Hayworth's office to cover the sum. It was sent back with a reply that they didn't know of 'such a contract.' An unheard of event where a managing agent refused extra money sent to them for a previously agreed contract. By refusing this money, it excused them of a requirement to provide extra staff. It seems quite obviously that McClelland was a token attendant sent to watch and 'check' the takings. Not mentioned by Hesseltine in his evidence, was that Graham the hall keeper was the next person to enter the scene of mayhem. He encountered some children at the bottom of the gallery stairs; this is his sworn evidence on what happened next,

Graham; they said they had been in the gallery, but that he (Hesseltine) would not give them any prizes. I got them off to the street via the gallery door, and in turning round I saw a number of children playing about in the lobby, and when I had cleared them out I went up the stairs, and on the first flight of the gallery stairs I saw a number of children coming down. Many of them had prizes in their hands, and I went up to get behind them and clear them out. When I got up to the door I saw it was partly open, and a man (Hesseltine) in the open space trying to pull some children out. I shouted, 'Man pull the door open.' I got no reply, I don't know whether he heard me, but I put my hand between his legs, reached round, and got hold of the bolt in the inside. I was unable to pull it out

Coroner; were there many children about then?

Graham; they were piled up to a great height inside. All the stairs so far as I could see were packed with children. I saw it was impossible to do any good where I was, and went round through the dress circle door, which was 'snecked' I succeeded in opening it. The pressure of the children made it difficult to open it. I strove to get the children out by this way, and with the help of others, several hundred children came out by way of this door.

That was about all the important evidence given with witnesses disagreeing on most things. Sunderland was holding its breath; perhaps the inquests could bring satisfactory answers to how 180 plus children could lose their lives at an entertainment especially planned for them. Would they be able to point a finger of retribution or would it be a finger of suspicion?

Chapter 12
Justice for the parents?

The Bishopwearmouth returned at six o'clock, when the Foreman said:

We find that Frederick Mills and others met their death by suffocation on the stairs leading from the gallery in the Victoria Hall on the 16th day of June, 1883, from the partial closing of a door on the landing, fixed in its position by a bolt in the floor, but by whom there is not sufficient evidence to show. That the manager of the entertainment be censured for not providing sufficient caretakers and assistants to preserve order in the hall on that afternoon, and we believe a partnership existed between Mr Coates and Mr Fay. That we consider the mode of entrance into, and of exits from the hall are sufficient, except the door at which the fatality occurred, and we would recommend its removal at once. We attach no blame to the caretaker, but recommend that in future the proprietor of the hall instruct him to show persons who engage the hall all its exits

The Monkwearmouth jury, dissatisfied with the result of the inquiry on the south side of the water, determined at a private meeting, held prior to their official sitting on the 9th July, to call certain witnesses who had not been previously examined.

The purpose of this was to discover new and fresh facts as to the cause of the disaster. Once the jury assembled in their official capacity, fourteen new witnesses, and several who had been already examined were summoned. After hearing their evidence nothing of importance was divulged. Following a two days' sitting the coroner summed up and the jury retired at five minutes past five o'clock, on the afternoon of Tuesday 10th July, to consider their verdict. They returned at a quarter past six, and through their foreman stated *that they found that Edith Ward and others met their death by suffocation through the partial closing and bolting of a door.*

They added that they did not know who had closed and bolted the door.

They then answered the questions set by the coroner. It was agreed that the responsibility of taking proper precautions, were that of Coates and Fay. They said that insufficient staff was provided to allow the children to depart from the gallery safely. They then pointed the finger at Graham by saying he had neglected his duty by not showing Fay and his assistants the existence of the door and by not bolting it back against the outer wall. They then criticised he directors of the Victoria Hall Company for erecting such an unusual door and not letting strangers know about it. The parents and teachers came under fire for not making sure that the children were kept safe. The coroner, after reading the verdict, asked the jury if they had decided whether the negligence of Fay and Coates was of a culpable character. The foreman replied *that the jury did not go to that length.*

The jury's foreman then read a statement.

We recommend that school children do not attend entertainments, treats, or excursions, except under proper supervision or control. We recommend that statutory powers ought to be forthwith applied to proprietors of buildings in which the public assemble, to provide at their own expense, and to the entire satisfaction of the municipal or local authorities, sufficient means of exit, all doors, both internal or external, to open outwards; proprietors' servants to be on duty on the premises from the commencement to the close of entertainments,

The door was the obvious reason why the accident happened and you would think that you would immediately introduce adequate measures so that a similar accident wouldn't happen again. It was generally accepted that the request of the Bishopwearmouth jury was that the fatal door should be burnt and that request was carried out. That was the end of the matter or so everybody thought, until a local newspaper reported.

It would appear that the other day a person went to inquire about the price of the door, and whether an offer for it would be accepted, and was told by agent of the proprietor of the hall that 100 guineas would be required. One of our reporters waited upon the proprietor of the hall (Mr. Frederick Taylor) yesterday morning, in the hope of obtaining an authoritative contradiction of report; but Taylor refused neither to contradict or confirm the statement, and seemed to resent the impertinence of the anxiety of the public, regarding the manner in which way he proposes to deal with this particular portion of 'His Property.'

The Victoria Hall accident was debated in the House of Commons on July 12 1883 after both inquests were finished. They seemed to consider that the teachers should carry the blame indicating how far off they were in distance and understanding.

The Day the Children Fell Asleep

Mr James asked the Vice President of the Council, If it was true as stated in the evidence at the recent inquest at Sunderland that the tickets for the fatal entertainment in the Victoria Hall were in certain cases distributed through elementary school teachers; whether any other similar cases have ever been brought under his notice; and, if he can take any steps to prevent a repetition of such a practice, by requesting managers to prohibit the circulation of tickets in elementary schools for entertainments where admission is only made by payment?

Vice President: I have inquired respecting the distribution of tickets for the entertainment at the Victoria Hall, Sunderland, and I find that advertisements not admission tickets were distributed by teachers in public elementary schools to the children under their charge. I regret to find that this practice has prevailed in the district for many years. I entirely concur in the censure conveyed in the presentment of the Jury at the Coroner's Inquest— That the masters of the various schools were not justified in allowing the children under their charge to be canvassed by Fay or their teachers, and the attendance of the children in effect secured, by free tickets being given to teachers, without some arrangement being made for the proper supervision and control of the children by teachers when at the entertainment. This seems to me a scandal and a breach of good order and discipline that our schools should be made the recruiting ground of itinerant conjurers, or the purveyors of any description of public entertainment. It is impossible to lay down rules for the guidance of local authorities, school managers, and teachers that shall be applicable in all circumstances and in every contingency. Moreover, there is great danger in attempting to do so, as it might be argued that what was not prohibited was permissible. I propose, however, to send a Circular to Her

Majesty's Inspectors calling their attention to what has happened in this case and to the verdict of the Jury, and instructing them to let it be known at the forthcoming inspections that any such invasion of the schools as I have referred to will be regarded as an infraction of the Code as it relates to discipline, and will be considered in the merit grant, and that children attending any school treat or entertainment of any description promoted by teachers or managers must do so under the care and guidance of their teachers.

There is no doubt that the outcome of the inquests resulted in bewilderment among some of the parents, who needed closure on the deaths. (That is if you can ever get closure for such deaths.) The decision reached, resulted in Fay and his manager being lightly reprimanded, for having a lack of assistants, to keep control in the hall. Hesseltine and Graham accused of lacking in care for the children. Graham for not informing Fay and his staff about the door. There is still the debate that even if the hall keeper had shown them the door, what difference would it have made? Teachers for allowing their pupils to attend a show where they couldn't ensure their safety, laying them open to *itinerant conjurers.* But no one charged, no one sent to prison, no one to face the wrath of the parents and the Sunderland population. One of the audience and taking special notice was Hans Lawrence who was a solicitors general clerk born in Sunderland in 1848. He was a distant relative of Elizabeth Ann Outlaw who said that Hans was at the inquests trying to understand how two of his children, Isobel 7 and John George 5, had left home on that summer's day yet failed to return, no peace or satisfaction for him. It would seem that there was certainly collusion with witnesses, which allowed the finger pointing at Graham regarding the infamous door. The same people who were in the hall for over five hours, yet completely denied any knowledge of it and by stating this, being able to deny any further knowledge of the bolt. It seemed they knew of every exit but didn't know of that particular door. In a more serious piece of evidence given by the hall proprietor, Frederick Taylor said, as much, *you* had to be blind not to realise that a door was there. As most of his evidence was lighthearted and at times untrue, was this one piece we can believe? Who opened it, who unbolted it from the outside wall? The children, Hesseltine? Who was responsible for it to become bolted to the floor? Or are we to believe it dropped in of its own accord. The inquests were loath to accept the children's evidence which pointed at Hesseltine placing the bolt in after clearing the hole with a piece of wood, or that he was heard to say to a girl leave the bolt alone. His constant feeling around the door as though seeking for a bolt he admitted he didn't know existed. The rush from the gallery was such that one man would be easily overcome forcing him down the stairs to the ever closing door and then his panic set in. The average height of a 22-year-old man in the late 1880s was less than five and a half feet. Hesseltine was not a big man. Fay tried to dismiss his responsibility from the lack of staff at the gallery by feebly saying he thought that Graham and his wife were still there. (Even though Graham was with him in the stalls.) This was said no doubt to lift blame on Mr Coates who had been sent up to assist in the distribution of prizes, yet didn't go immediately. Coates later admitted he couldn't go as he was looking after the money. Who did he give the money to when he was supposedly at the door-rescuing children? Coates also said he saw children exiting from the gallery with toys, yet still didn't notice the door.

We must not forget that after the funerals and the media attention, the parents were left with the empty silence of missing children. The agony of losing a child of any age is unparalleled and the parent's memory is frozen in time to when they opened their front door and let out their children. There is no age or point in time that makes it any easier, no parent expects to face the death of their child and no grandparent expects to bury their grandchild. The death of a child goes against the natural order we expect life to follow. The loss carries with it the loss of the future, the hopes, dreams, and potential that can never be fulfilled. The longing for the child and the feeling of emptiness can last a lifetime. Some parents describe feeling complete disbelief, mixed with flashes of reality, too awful to think about. They feel numb, empty, enraged, anxious or exhausted. A feeling of guilt surrounds them that they were responsible for their safety and that as a parent should have been able to prevent what happened. There may be nothing they could have done differently, but such feelings can be strong and can be replayed over and over again as they tried to make sense of what had happened. The endless days of looking around for them, allocating tasks to missing children that they will never carry out. Consoling their sons and daughters who survived the crush, who are now guilt ridden because they didn't save the sisters, brothers and friends that went with them on that bright summer day. How did they carry on with the daily routine of family life? Or even move forward in their lives. Many women just couldn't and retreated into their memories, with their husbands also suffering, watching on in despair. Parents from a religious background may feel that the death is a punishment for a sin or transgression. That God is punishing them, as one local paper rather dramatically likened the disaster to the first born being killed by Herod. The loss of a sister or a brother despite the fact they might belong to a large family is devastating for the ones left. Children aged between 5 and 10 worry that others may die too and need constant reassuring that everything will be all right. They become withdrawn or liable to lose their tempers, over trivial events and have problems sleeping. Siblings may have to compete with idealised images of the dead sister or brother. (Your sister wouldn't have done that etc.) The calamity which the family never forget, causing members to remind everyone that 'Anne would have been twelve today.'

Bereavement, which has been described as being a sickness without a simple solution. It can be said that many siblings of those who died were shortly afterwards taken ill and many children were frightened by gatherings of large crowds or the closeness of school classrooms. Some, still feeling the moment a hand slipped from theirs, resulting in them clinging to their parents for safety. Obviously some of the parents and children were suffering with a type of posttraumatic stress that was not recognised by doctors of the time. Many of the parents were told to pull themselves together and get on with it. That is what they tried to do; these were tough hardy people who deserved better and yet were abused by the people who should have been helping them. Accusing them of greed and wanting to gain from the deaths of their children. Their saviour was the closeness of families who lived nearby who had also had children killed. At the time many streets carried the echo of the dead children, who would have been playing outside and knocking for playmates, the whole area were witnesses to grief. Uncles, aunts and cousins all within touching distance and ready to supply assistance to the bereaved. Workplaces of the parents were filled with empathy and condolences for their work pals.

How long does grief last? Many studies have been carried out without a definite answer. The time course for parental grief is uncertain and can be expected to show great variability.

Traditional models that described *the grief response*, proposed that grief reactions should be completed within a few weeks to a few months after a death. However, research has suggested that a more typical time line of grief begins with shock and intense grief for 2 weeks, followed by 2 months of strong grieving, and then a slow recovery that takes about 2 years. Others have indicated that even this time line is too short in the situation of a child's death. They have found that parents reported thinking of the death of their child daily 3 and 4 years after the event, also, emotional ties to deceased children may not be fully severed, and negative emotions might persist despite other forms of positive adaptation. Thus, many parents grieve indefinitely. Not having a conclusive verdict of who was responsible and how it came about that their children were left to die in such terrible circumstances. Unfortunately the building remained standing, providing the survivors with a daily reminder of where the children's lives ended.

Despite the accusing finger being pointed at Graham, the majority of Sunderland folk held him in great respect. At the inquest a juryman interrupted the coroner's questioning of Graham accusing him of *talking to him as if he was a criminal.* Showing support for Frederick Graham were letters to the Editor of the Sunderland Echo

It is rather late in the day to refer, for the hundredth time, to the above catastrophe, but having been from home for several weeks since it happened was interested enough, after my return, personally and minutely to investigate its causes and consequences, its horrors and its alleviations, and was astonished to find that the chief agent in preventing much greater sacrifice of life than actually took place had received no public recognition, honour, or reward. I refer to the caretaker of the hall, who besides, and by means of, the rescue just mentioned, exposed himself to serious danger, and actually suffered both in mind and body considerable extent. Unprompted, sir, by him or anyone else, but by my own reflections, desire your columns to ask the following questions:

1. Is it not true that but for the caretaker's arresting cataract of children on the lauding before the fatal stairs, and diverting the torrent through the door leading into the dress circle area a much greater sacrifice of life would have occurred

2nd. Is it not true that forcing his way to the said stairs, through the dying and the dead, he saved at the last moment several of these from the fate of lost companions

3rd Is it not true that, effecting this rescue, he stood and struggled in the midst of deadly stench by which he was half suffocated, and which very few men could have endured?

4th. Is it not true that he has been acquitted in a lawful Court of all blame this calamity

5th. Is it not true that he was the first to send messenger for the doctors, who so promptly responded to the call, and so gallantly co-operated the work of rescue and restoration If, sir, these things are true and I challenge contradiction to appeal to the public, and especially the parents of the saved children, honorable to allow this humble, and self denying benefactor to sink into oblivion, unthanked and unrewarded There has been, I hear, much squabbling about the use of the money contributed from all quarters to alleviate the misery caused by this disaster, but I think that most of the kind donors, if they had been acquainted with the facts above enumerated, would have been only too glad see a part of their liberality, awarded to the saviour of Victoria Hal —l am, sir, yours truly, A Senior Minister

John Taylor

> Sir, I find that very erroneous notions are held by the public with regard to the duties of hall keepers, and consequently some unpleasant and unjust remarks have been made regarding Mr Graham, the care-taker of the Victoria Hall, in connection with the terrible disaster that has thrown the country into mourning. My experience during nearly thirty years of public life is as follows: Caretakers usually open the door doors of the hall at the time announced for opening, though this is not really part of their duty, and close them again after the audience has left. And this is all the tenant or entertainer can legitimately demand, excepting other arrangements have been 'made with the caretaker or the agent of the hall soon at the entertainer takes possession it is his duty to see to all internal arrangements, and to appoint some person to attend to the doors of egress, and to open them before dismisses the audience. Mr Graham had no business with the fatal" door, and commonsense supports my view as well as experience

But not everyone had kind words to those he considered to be responsible for looking after the children in the hall. This letter appeared in the Echo in July

> Since the terrible event of June I have had many keen cuts both from newspaper articles and from Job's comforters whom I have chanced to meet in the streets, but the keenest cut all appears in your paper of Thursday's date, written by some person who is ashamed of his name. But cowards always skulk behind a nom de plume and I would venture to say that "Townsman" had no child suffocated behind that fatal door. Through him, he now seeks to make a martyr of and give a reward to the hall keeper. I had not intended to write one line about this dreadful affair, but seeing the apparent desire of "Townsman" to give recompense to Mr F. Graham for his inattention at the hall on the 16th June, I

would suggest that "Townsman" should personally canvass the bereaved families for this object, and call at 126, first— Yours, Ac., R. H. Watson. 126, Wayman-Street.

Mr Watson lost three children in the crush, and one can understand his anger although not completely agree with his view. There were many letters sent, none as strange as this communication sent in supposedly by the private secretary of the President of the Irish Republic (pro tem)

Sir I am directed by The President of the Irish Republic (pro-tem) to convey to you the expression of his sincere regret at the calamity which has befallen the inhabitants of Sunderland.

Fortunately the day has passed, if there ever was, when the people of Ireland could discern in the misfortune the hand of an avenging deity, who, incensed at the judicial murders committed in their midst by a self imposed and illegal government has opened the gates of darkness upon the people of England and poring vials of his just wrath upon them, has made the children suffer for the sins of their of their Fathers. Moved, then, by the better spirit, which is beginning to pervade humanity. The President pro-tem, forgetting for the moment past and present wrongs endured at the hands of the English Government, kneels with your people in this hour of anguish and cries with them in all humility to the one father of all, that he may look upon them with mercy and pour his healing balm into their hearts.

I have the honour, sir, to remain your obedient servant, E. Mindful.

This letter must be taken with a pinch of salt and I think Ever Mindful is the clue. It would seem to be a bit of mischief to get people to focus on the home rule for the Irish campaign, which was receiving major media attention at the time.

To reinforce the belief that Mr Graham was innocent of any crimes was endorsed by the recognition for services rendered when the calamity occurred. Frederick Graham received a testimonial. It was presented at The Central Coffee Tavern in the High street The Gospel-Temperance Band also attended and played several selections of music. The presentation, which had been subscribed to by over 400 people, took the shape of a handsome marble time-piece, bearing the following inscription; Presented to Frederick Graham by public subscriptions for his efforts in saving life at the Victoria Ball disaster on June 16th, also, a gold star with a medallion in the centre, with on one side a figure of the hall in relief. The Mayor, in making the presentation, said he knew Mr. Graham before he was caretaker of the hall. He spoke of his great diligence in the discharge of his duties while in connection with the hall. The calamity would have been more agonising in its facts but for the timely interposition of Graham. This remark brought applause and he did not suppose that on that night his services would be rewarded afterwards. He added that Mr. Graham could not have been more grateful towards his fellow-townsmen who had given expression to their appreciation in very marked and tangible a manner.

Graham in response said that while he proud to receive such a testimonial, no man could forget the circumstances, which brought him to be standing here. Councilor Surtees concluded the proceedings by recognisng the honesty with which Mr. Graham had performed his duties in connection with the hall.

No doubt the whole affair had a lasting effect on Frederick, his wife and family so it comes with no surprise that Frederick Graham left Victoria Hall a few years later. In 1891 census he had moved to Clanny Street. By 1901 census he and his wife were found at 13 Brougham Street where he was employed as a paint shop assistant. In both streets he came in contact with many children he had saved from the crush. He died in 1910. His son Victor Hall became a shipwright and had 3 daughters and one son. In 1939 Victor was employed as a property repairer, he was still based in Sunderland at Shakespeare Terrace. This is where he died aged 74; during his life he had a close connection with the Salvation Army. His sister married young and I have not found any trace of her.

Over the eleven years that had passed since the Victoria hall tragedy, saw the rest of the money finally given away to the convalescent home developments with the committees shedding themselves of a colossal headache. The girls who survived the incident were now married, with attention seeking children of their own. The bereaved mothers without the help of birth control conceived more children. Other events in Sunderland had caused the memory of that day to slightly diminish but not for the families directly involved. Those children who, but for the unfortunate event on that sunny afternoon, could have worn the shirt of Sunderland Football club and became a terrace hero. Could have been getting ready for another shift in the factory. They may have been leaders in the support for the rights of woman and in gaining the vote. They could have been solicitors, writers, or acclaimed artists. Dreams and ambitions all wiped out in ten minutes of distracted madness. These were children, who when grown, were capable of contributing something worthwhile, constructive and warmth to Sunderland's society. Alexander Fay went back to Tynemouth and continued to give shows. There isn't any evidence that he gave any more children shows and is reported to have died in the Leeds workhouse poverty. (I have found no record of this but could be listed under another name)

The memorial statue, many agree, should be set in the Sunderland museum to protect it from any further damage. It is a lasting memorial to those unfortunate children and should be looked after.

Albert Anderson wrote in his book

For those who had lost children in the Victoria Hall Disaster the building was a constant reminder of that dreadful day. The Alexander Hall extension altered the appearance but it was still the same place that had claimed their little ones. During the Second World War, Sunderland was a large shipbuilding town and was a prime target for German bombers. During an air raid on the night of 15/16th of April the Luftwaffe dropped a parachute mines on the town for the first time. One landed in Laura Street the explosion leveled most of Victoria Hall that the remains had to be demolished.

This calamity is now a distant memory nearly 140 years ago. We must be encouraged to visit the memorial statue and stand and pay our respects to these children. I'm sure Sunderland will appreciate that and no doubt so will the children.

※※※

Chapter 13
Poems dedicated to the disaster

'Twas in the town of Sunderland, and in the year of 1883,
That about 200 children were launch'd into eternity
While witnessing an entertainment in Victoria Hall,
While they, poor little innocents, to God for help did call.
The entertainment consisted of conjuring, and the ghost illusion play,
Also talking waxworks, and living marionettes, and given by Mr Fay;
And on this occasion, presents were to be given away,
But in their anxiety of getting presents they wouldn't brook delay,
And that is the reason why so many lives have been taken away;
But I hope their precious souls are in heaven to-day.

As soon as the children began to suspect
that they would lose their presents by neglect,
they rush'd from the gallery, and ran down the stairs pell-mell,
and trampled one another to death, according as they fell.

John Taylor

As soon as the catastrophe became known throughout the boro'
the people's hearts were brim-full of sorrow,
and parents rush'd to the Hall terror-stricken and wild,
and each one was anxious to find their own child.

Oh! it must have been a most horrible sight.
To see the dear little children struggling with all their might
To get out at the door at the foot of the stair,
While one brave little boy did repeat the Lord's Prayer.

The innocent children were buried seven or eight layers deep,
The sight was heart-rending and enough to make one weep;
It was a most affecting spectacle and frightful to behold
The corpse of a little boy not above four years old,

Who had on a top-coat much too big for him,
And his little innocent face was white and grim,
And appearing to be simply in a calm sleep-
The sight was enough to make one's flesh to creep.

The scene in the Hall was heart sickening to behold,
and enough to make one's blood run cold.
To see the children's faces, blackened, that were trampled to death,
and their parents lamenting o'er them with bated breath.

Oh! it was most lamentable for to hear
The cries of the mothers for their children dear;
And many mothers swooned in grief away
At the sight of their dead children in grim array.

The Day the Children Fell Asleep

There was a parent took home a boy by mistake,
And after arriving there his heart was like to break
When it was found to be the body of a neighbour's child;
The parent stood aghast and was like to go wild.

A man and his wife rush'd madly in the Hall,
And loudly in grief on their children they did call,
And the man searched for his children among the dead
Seemingly without the least fear or dread.

And with his finger pointing he cried. "That's one! two!
Oh! heaven above, what shall I do;"
And still he kept walking on and murmuring very low.
Until he came to the last child in the row;

then he cried, "Good God! All my family gone
And now I am left to mourn alone;"
And staggering back he cried, "Give me water, give me water!"
While his heart was like to break and his teeth seem'd to chatter.

Oh, heaven! It must have been most pitiful to see
Fathers with their dead children upon their knee
While the blood ran copiously from their mouths and ears
And their parents shedding o'er them hot burning tears.

I hope the Lord will comfort their parents by night and by day,
For He gives us life and He takes it away,
Therefore I hope their parents will put their trust in Him,
because to weep for the dead it is a sin.

Her Majesty's grief for the bereaved parents has been profound,
And I'm glad to see that she has sent them £50;
And I hope from all parts of the world will flow relief
To aid and comfort the bereaved parents in their grief.

William Topaz McGonagall

I did warn you that this would be a typical Victorian ode. He was described by one of his critics as being 'The Worst Victorian Poet but there again how can you brighten up a calamity such as this. In America they tried.

Top of Form
But bleeds for you mothers of the north
And strong men groan in sorrow for your case
Yet hearten up your loss is but for time
Eternity shall give your darlings back to you
And mid your raining tears
Take this one thought to heart
Your little ones have got safely home
And have all won their prizes.
The Detroit free press 1883

Angels of Sunderland
They danced and they shouted full of glee.
They rushed to find out what the presents could be
And the sea of young faces were borne along
Until checked by a barrier stout and strong
Then the bright current was brought to a stand
And a heart-piecing shriek rang through Sunderland.

The Day the Children Fell Asleep

Who can give comfort in grief such as this
Man's arm is helpless no power in his
There is but one unto whom we can find
One who in mercy cries come unto me
One who in pity outstretches his hand
To the heartbroken mourners of Sunderland.

The last verse is
Sad will the homes be for many a day.
Where the light of the household has been snatched away
But through the dull cloud of sorrow and pain
Shines the hope that at last we may meet them again
For on the bright shores of the better land
Are gathered the treasures of SUNDERLAND.
E.C. Nicholson

Morning in the school
but where the cheery noise?
Why do teachers crowd and whisper low?
Who was sobbing are those all the boys?
Is that the master voice so choked and low?
Unknown

184 beloved little ones
How many a home is filled with grief
How many a sigh we hear
As down each pale and care worn cheek
Descends a little tear
The happy looks, the beaming smile
Of children young and gay

No more will cheer the parent's heart
For ever passed away
Oh! Thou who once didst children bless
Whilst sojourning below
Design to assuage the bosom's grief
And dry the tears that flow
And whisper to each suffering form
The words that joy shall give
Though passed away from earthly scenes
In brighter ones they live.
L M Thornton

This was taken from a memorial card dedicated to the disaster.
A wail of deep sorrow thrills over the land
And scatters distraction on every hand
Poor fathers and mothers their hearts have been wrung
And bitter lament burst from every tongue.

Strong arms soon were ready and willing to save
But alas near 200 sleep in their grave
And the voices of parents distracted with fears
Cried aloud in the depth of their anguish and tears

It continues with lines such as 'Tear sprinkled wreaths '

It must have been an earlier poem as it states 200 children killed a total given before the funerals. The author is unknown but for the initials J.H.

The full poem can be viewed in Marie Gardiner's book Secret Sunderland.

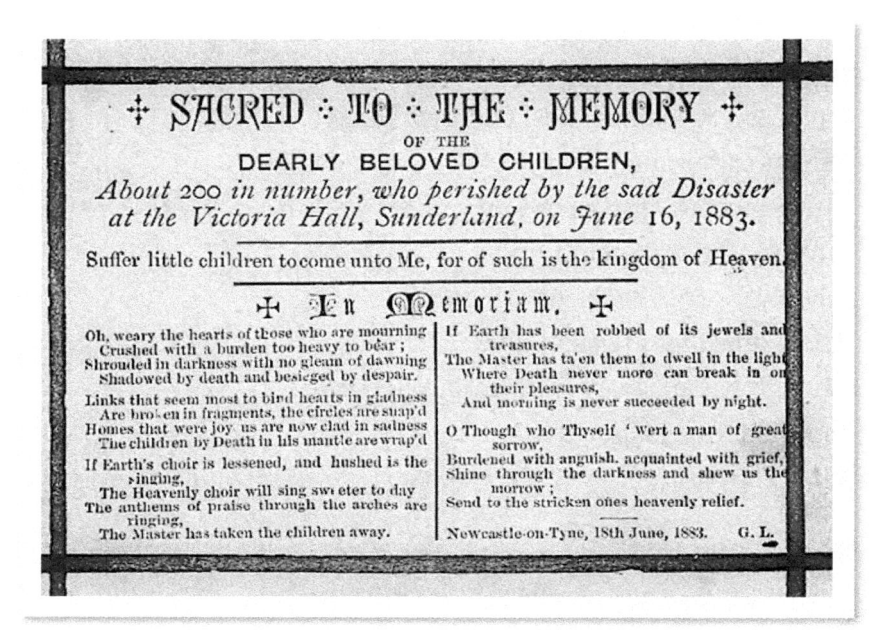

> ✣ **SACRED ∵ TO ∵ THE ∵ MEMORY** ✣
> OF THE
> **DEARLY BELOVED CHILDREN,**
> *About 200 in number, who perished by the sad Disaster at the Victoria Hall, Sunderland, on June 16, 1883.*
>
> Suffer little children to come unto Me, for of such is the kingdom of Heaven.
>
> ✣ **In Memoriam.** ✣
>
> Oh, weary the hearts of those who are mourning
> Crushed with a burden too heavy to bear;
> Shrouded in darkness with no gleam of dawning
> Shadowed by death and besieged by despair.
>
> Links that seem most to bind hearts in gladness
> Are broken in fragments, the circles are snap'd
> Homes that were joy us are now clad in sadness
> The children by Death in his mantle are wrap'd
>
> If Earth's choir is lessened, and hushed is the singing,
> The Heavenly choir will sing sweeter to day
> The anthems of praise through the arches are ringing,
> The Master has taken the children away.
>
> If Earth has been robbed of its jewels and treasures,
> The Master has ta'en them to dwell in the light
> Where Death never more can break in on their pleasures,
> And morning is never succeeded by night.
>
> O Though who Thyself 'Wert a man of great sorrow,
> Burdened with anguish, acquainted with grief,
> Shine through the darkness and shew us the morrow;
> Send to the stricken ones heavenly relief.
>
> Newcastle-on-Tyne, 18th June, 1883.   G. L.

Another early poem as it states 200 perished. This was printed on a 'mourning card' issued on 18th June, evidently from Newcastle.

There was even a musical stage show based on the disaster, which premiered in the Sunderland Empire on May 6th 2005. It was called a Cry in the Dark and was written by Fiona Clegg who directed choreographed and starred in the show. It was described *as moving and powerful, an experience not to be missed.*

I'm sorry but I think I will pass on that.

Margaret a relation of the Victoria Hall caretaker Frederick Graham

I first got in touch with Margaret after I read her story in the Sunderland Echo, which I include below.

Growing up in post war Sunderland I was aware of the bombsites that scarred the town centre. There was a particularly large one by the station and many smaller ones. One of these was next to the office of the Corporation Parks Department, which I occasionally visited with my father who was employed by the department. This was at the junction of Toward Road and Laura Street and had been the site of the Victoria Hall until a German parachute mine destroyed it on the night of the 15th /16th April 1941.

The Day the Children Fell Asleep

Victoria Hall, Sunderland,
On Saturday Afternoon at 3 o'clock.
SCHOOL TICKET

THE FAYS

From the Tynemouth Aquarium,
Will give a Grand Day Performance for Children,
THE GREATEST TREAT FOR CHILDREN EVER GIVEN
Conjuring, Talking Waxworks, Living Marionettes, The Great Ghost Illusion, &c.

This Ticket will admit any number of Children on payment of
ONE PENNY Each; Reserved Seats, 3d., Nurses or Parents with Children 3d.

PRIZES!

Every Child entering the room will stand a chance of receiving a handsome Present, Books, Toys, &c.

This Entertainment has been witnessed by thousands of delighted Children throughout England.

As a child I knew about the tragic deaths of many children at the hall on Saturday 16th June 1883 following an entertainment by the Fays, who were based at Tynemouth. Various acts were to perform and each child was to be given a present at the end of the show. Leaflets advertising the "greatest treat for children ever given" were distributed via many schools in Sunderland, I don't remember if I learned of this disaster at school or from my parents but it was an important event in the history of Sunderland.

Many years later I began to research my Sunderland roots. I knew my great great grandfather was Joseph Graham and his wife was Mary Ann nee English. Joseph was a Baptist Minister at Hallgarth Square Chapel, which he had helped to build. I suspect that he had little or no income from his ministry so he supported his family by teaching and later business dealings. He is listed as a timber merchant in the 1850's voters lists for Monkwearmouth and in the 1861 census. Joseph's timber business went bankrupt after supplying a well-known local shipbuilder who failed to pay his bills. He died on May 29th 1862.

The sons of Mary and Joseph had various forms of employment but two of them, Joseph and Frederick, were employed in their father's timber yard in 1861. After the bankruptcy they obviously had to find alternative employment. I followed the Grahams through various censuses and was surprised by what I found in 1881. Frederick Graham was recorded as the manager of the Victoria Hall and he was living on the premises in Toward Road with his wife Jane Ann nee Charlton and his two children, a daughter born in 1867 and a son born in 1873.

Tess Newton related to the Vowell sisters

Grace and Lily both died in the crush; their brother Joseph identified their bodies. Their two brothers Thomas and Chapman were at the entertainment and luckily survived. The two boys attended their school on the Monday after the tragedy to the surprise of their teachers, who had been told that they had both died. Chapman unfortunately was badly affected by what he had seen and endured; he sadly died three years later. The Family were living at 5 Norfolk Street at the time, which they shared with Miss Atkinson who we are told 'Sold the finest china in town.' The Embassies of Portugal, Brazil and Spain were situated in this street. This reflected the trade being carried out in Sunderland in the late 19c. Nearby was a grocer, which was listed as Thomas's occupation in a later census. Tess, who lives in Australia, sent me an e-mail, which I include below.

The Vowell sisters are the daughters of my great great grandfather's youngest sister Jane Newton/Vowell. The Newton family first immigrated to Australia in 1879 where my grandfather Robert Newton son of James Newton and my great Grandmother Sarah Archer/Newton, who were both from Newcastle, settled in South Australia, later moving to New South Wales.

The census of 1881 of the Vowell family

VOWELL, David C	47	Head	Mar	Coppersmith	NBL: Ncastle	1834
VOWELL, Jane	46	Wife	Mar	Coppersmiths Wife	DUR: Gateshead	1835
VOWELL, William	23	Son	Unn	Brass Moulder	DUR: Gateshead	1858
VOWELL, Margaret	21	Dau	Unn	Domestic (Serv)	DUR: Gateshead	1860
VOWELL, Joseph	13	Son		Scholar	NBL: Ncastle	1868

VOWELL, Chapman	10	Son		Scholar	NBL: Ncastle	1871
VOWELL, Thomas	8	Son		Scholar	DUR: Stockton	1873
VOWELL, Grace N.	6	Dau		Scholar	DUR: Stockton	1875
VOWELL, Lilly	2	Dau			DUR: Srland	1879

Emanuel Musgrove Gibson, the brother of John George who died in the crush. Their father, John an Engine Fitter, identified his son on the floor of the theatre's dress circle.

The Day the Children Fell Asleep

Below is Mark Gibson who is the great grandson of Emanuel.

Printed by permission of Mark Gibson

Note that cause of death is listed as death by suffocation on Gallery stairs by partial closing of door. The Registrar then adds, *by whom, no evidence*. Mark obtained the certificate when he was tracing his family history. He was fascinated by the reason for death trying to understand how a partial opening of a door could be responsible. We got in touch via a Durham website and he gave me permission to include it in this book. How raw this must have felt to the parents reading it, with no satisfaction for them. Every child who died must have been issued with similar death certificates that mirrored the cause. The formidable parents of Sunderland must have felt frustrated with the outcome of the inquest and present day genealogist baffled by the remarks of the death certificates.

ঌঌঌ